Codependency Recovery Guide

Cure your Codependent Personality & Relationships with this No More Codependence User Manual, Heal from Narcissists & Sociopathic People by Learning How to Take Back Control

By Victoria Hoffman

Table of Contents

Codependency Recovery Guide
Table of Contents
Introduction
Chapter 1 – Are you Codependent?

- The Traits of Codependency
- How Codependency Develops

Codependency Tests
Chapter 2 – Revisiting Your Past

- Dysfunctional Families
- Addiction
- Illnesses

Chapter 3 – The Recovery Process

- Setting Boundaries
- Putting Yourself First
- Listen to Others
- Validation

Chapter 4 – Break the Patterns

- Denial
- Low Self-Esteem
- Compliance
- Control
- Avoidance
- Recovery Reminders

Conclusion

Introduction

Congratulations on purchasing the *Codependency Recovery Guide* and thank you for doing so.

The following chapters will discuss the different approaches towards recovering from a codependent relationship and the best ways of rebuilding your life once again. There are lots of practical examples that can be followed to help an individual recover from a bad relationship or rebuild their existing love.

There are plenty of books on this subject on the market, thanks again for choosing this one! Every effort was made to ensure it is full of as much useful information as possible, please enjoy it!

Chapter 1 – Are you Codependent?

Codependency is a dysfunctional relationship where an individual relies on the other(s) for their emotional and passionate needs. It likewise portrays a relationship that empowers someone else to keep up their flippant, addictive, or underachieving conduct.

Do you feel caught in your relationship? Is it accurate to say that you are the one that is always making sacrifices in your relationship? At that point, you might be in a codependent relationship.

The term codependency has been around for a considerable length of time. In spite of the fact that it initially applied to life partners of heavy drinkers (first called co-drunkards), specialists uncovered that the attributes of codependents were considerably more pervasive in the all-inclusive community than had recently envisioned. Truth be told, they found that if you were brought up in a dysfunctional family or had an evil parent, you could likewise be codependent.

Specialists likewise found that codependent side effects deteriorated if left untreated. Fortunately, they're reversible.

Manifestations of Codependency

Coming up next is a rundown of indications of codependency and being in a codependent relationship. You do not need them all to qualify as codependent.

Dysfunctional correspondence. Codependents experience difficulty with regard to imparting their considerations, emotions, and requirements. Obviously, if you do not have a clue of what you think, feel, or need, this turns into an issue. You are hesitant to be honest, on the grounds that you would prefer not to annoy another person. Communication winds up untrustworthy and confounding when you attempt to control the other individual out of dread.

Poor limits. Limits are kind of a nonexistent line among you and others. It splits what's yours and someone else's, and that applies not exclusively to your body, cash, and possessions, but also to your emotions, contemplations, and necessities. That is particularly hard for codependents. They have foggy or frail limits. They feel in charge of other individuals' emotions and issues or fault their very own on another person. Some codependents have inflexible limits. They are deterred and pulled back, making it difficult for other individuals to draw near to them. Some of the time, individuals flip to and fro between having feeble limits and having inflexible ones.

Rejection. One of the issues individuals face in getting help for codependency is that they're trying to claim ignorance about it, implying that they do not confront their concern. Typically, they think the issue is another person or the circumstance. They either continue whining or attempting to fix the other individual or move between various relationships or jobs and never confess up the way that they have an issue. Codependents likewise deny their sentiments and necessities. Frequently, they do not have the foggiest idea of what they're feeling and are rather centered around what others are feeling. Something very similar goes for their needs. They focus on other individuals' needs and not their own. They may be trying to claim ignorance of their requirement for space and self-governance. Albeit some codependents appear to be penniless, others act like they're independent with regards to requiring help. They will not connect and experience difficulty getting attention. They are willfully ignorant of their helplessness and requirement for adoration and closeness.

Reactivity. A result of poor limits is that you respond to everybody's contemplations and emotions. If somebody says something you cannot help contradicting, you either trust it or become protective. You ingest their words, on the grounds that there is no limit. With a limit, you would understand it was only their assessment and not an impression of you and not feel compromised by differences.

Caretaking. Another impact of poor limits is that if another person has an issue, you need to push them to the point that you surrender yourself. It is normal to feel compassion toward somebody, however, codependents start putting other individuals in front of themselves. Indeed, they have to help and may feel rejected if someone else doesn't need assistance. In addition, they continue attempting to help and fix the other individual, notwithstanding when that individual unmistakably is not taking their recommendation.

Low confidence. Feeling that you are bad enough or contrasting yourself with others are indications of low confidence. The dubious thing about confidence is that a few people have a favorable opinion of themselves, yet, it is just a mask — they really feel unlovable or lacking. Underneath, typically avoided cognizance, are sentiments of disgrace. Blame and hairsplitting regularly oblige low confidence. If everything is immaculate, you do not feel terrible about yourself.

Control. Control helps codependents have a sense of security. Everybody needs some authority over occasions in their life. You wouldn't have any desire to live in steady vulnerability and disorder, however, for codependents, control restrains their capacity to go out on a limb and offer their sentiments. Some of the time, they have an addiction that either causes them to extricate up, similar to liquor abuse, or encourages them to hold their emotions down, similar to workaholism, with the goal that they do not show it. Codependents additionally need to control those near them, since they need other individuals to carry on with a particular goal in mind to feel OK. It is possible to have programs that help individuals understand how to control themselves. Then again, codependents are bossy and reveal to you what you ought to or shouldn't do. This is an infringement of another person's limit.

Difficult feelings. Codependency makes pressure and prompts agonizing feelings. Disgrace and low confidence make uneasiness and dread about being judged, dismissed, committing errors, being a disappointment, and feeling caught by being close or being separated from everyone else. Different side effects lead to sentiments of indignation and disdain, despondency, misery, and hopelessness. At the point when the emotions are excessive, you can feel numb.

Satisfying others. It is fine to need to satisfy somebody you care about, however, codependents ordinarily do not think they have a decision. Saying "No" causes them uneasiness. Some codependents experience serious difficulties saying "No" to anybody. They make a special effort and sacrifice their own needs to suit other individuals.

Reliance. Codependents need other individuals to like them to feel okay about themselves. They're anxious about being rejected or deserted, regardless of whether they can work individually. There are people who constantly need the approval of others even when it is better to think for themselves. This quality makes it difficult for them to cut off an association even when a relationship is not working out for them.

Issues with closeness. By this, it is the problems associated with being intimate with your partner. I'm looking at being open and close with somebody in a private relationship. As a result of feeling afraid, you may expect that you'll be judged, rejected, or left. partnerpartnerSome people feel that their partners are way more sophisticated than them and, in turn, fear to share their actual lives with them. This is a serious problem that can persist for a long time in a relationship and cause unexpected damage.

There is help for recuperation and change for individuals who are codependent. The initial step is getting direction from a close friend or family member and get the process started. It is better to do it immediately than wait.

The Traits of Codependency

Think about codependency—when two individuals with dysfunctional characteristics become more terrible together. Enmeshment happens when clear limits about where you start and where your partner finishes are not plainly characterized.

Think about the most despondent couple you have at any point met. (Ideally, you are not a piece of this pair.) You may ask why these individuals are still attached. Grown-ups are willing members in organizations. What's more, as unfortunate as connections might be, there can be gains for the two gatherings. Basic purposes behind staying together incorporate youngsters, accounts, time contributed, and dread of the disgrace that may accompany separating. Yet, the greater issue is the conviction that one or the two individuals accept they have the right to be abused.

Indications of Codependency

The customary meaning of codependency has concentrated on control, support, and upkeep of associations with people who are artificially reliant, or participating in unfortunate practices, for example, narcissism. An exemplary codependency model is an alcoholic spouse and his empowering wife.

Scientists contend that codependent people share the duty regarding the unfortunate conduct, principally by concentrating their lives on the wiped out or the terrible conduct and by making their very own confidence and prosperity depend upon the conduct of the undesirable relative.

Different scientists guessed that the practical (or sound) partner supports the distressed partner when the individual takes part in unwanted conduct. This conduct is at last wonderful to the distressed partner, which serves to fortify it. The partner who controls the most rewards (which manufactures their capacity base) is thought to be the amazing one, while the other is obliged to the person in question. At whatever point there is progressing struggle, there is basic understanding. As such, it takes two to tango, and the needy or subservient partner may not be as powerless, aloof, or blameless as they show up.

The accompanying inquiries can fill in as a manual to decide whether your relationship includes codependency:

- Do you spread your partner's issues with medications, liquor, or the law?
- Does your feeling of direction include making outrageous sacrifices to fulfill your partner's needs?
- Do you stay silent to maintain a strategic distance from contentions?
- Do you continually stress over others' assessments of you?
- Do you feel caught in your relationship?
- Is it difficult to state no when your partner makes requests on your time and life?

The Development of Codependency

During childbirth, we are characteristically helpless and totally subject to our guardians for nourishment, security, and guideline. A newborn child's connection and clinging to at least one parental figure is basic for physical and enthusiastic survival. This basic connection makes the newborn child dependent on the necessities and vulnerabilities of the parental figure.

Growing up with a problematic or inaccessible parent means assuming the job of overseer and additionally empowering agent. A youngster, in this circumstance, puts the parent's needs first.

Dysfunctional families do not recognize that issues exist. Accordingly, its individuals quell feelings and neglect their own needs to concentrate on the necessities of the inaccessible parent(s). At the point when the "parentified" youngster turns into a grown-up, the individual in question rehashes a similar dynamic in their grown-up connections.

Disdain fabricates when you do not perceive your very own wants and needs. A typical conduct inclination is to blow up or lash out when your partner allows you to down. Coming up short on an interior locus of control means looking for outer wellsprings of approval and control. You may attempt to control your partner's practices so you can feel OK. You may act bombastic and bossy, and make irrational requests on your partner. Furthermore, when you understand you cannot control their dispositions or activities you become disillusioned, and may slide into a discouraged state.

It tends to be difficult to recognize an individual who is codependent and one who is simply tenacious or fascinated with someone else. Be that as it may, an individual who is codependent will typically:

- Remain in the relationship regardless of whether they know that their partner does destructive things.

- Discover no fulfillment or joy in life outside of getting things done for the other individual.

- Utilize all their time and vitality to give their partner all that they request.

- Overlook their own ethics or inner voice to do what the other individual needs.

- Feel consistent nervousness about their relationship because of their longing to consistently be fulfilling to the other individual.

- Do anything to please and fulfill their empowering agent regardless of the cost to themselves.

- Other individuals may attempt to converse with the codependent about their worries. In any case, regardless of whether others propose that the individual is excessively needy, an individual in a codependent relationship will think that it is difficult to leave the relationship.

- Feel regretful about considering themselves in the relationship and will not express any needs or wants.

- The codependent individual will feel extraordinary clash about isolating themselves from the empowering agent on the grounds that their own character is focused after sacrificing themselves for the other individual.

How Codependency Develops

Codependency is something that can be passed down from one generation to another. It is a passionate and conduct condition that influences a person's capacity to have a sound, commonly fulfilling relationship. It is otherwise called "relationship addiction" since individuals with codependency frequently structure or keep up connections that are uneven, sincerely damaging as well as injurious. The turmoil was first identified around ten years back as the aftereffect of long periods of considering relational connections in groups of drunkards. Mutually dependent conduct is found out by watching and impersonating other relatives who show this sort of conduct.

Who Does Co-Dependency Affect?

Codependency frequently influences a life partner, a parent, kin, companion, or collaborator of an individual harassed with liquor or medication reliance. Initially, mutually dependent was a term used to depict partners in concoction reliance, people living with, or in an association with an addicted individual. Comparative examples have been found in individuals involved with incessantly or rationally sick people. Today, be that as it may, the term has expanded to portray any mutually dependent individual from any dysfunctional family.

What is a Dysfunctional Family and How does it Lead to Co-Dependency?

A dysfunctional family is one in which individuals experience the ill effects of dread, outrage, torment, or disgrace that is overlooked or denied. Basic issues may incorporate any of the accompanyings:

- An addiction by a relative to drugs, liquor, connections, work, nourishment, sex, or betting.

- The presence of physical, passionate, or sexual maltreatment.

- The nearness of a relative experiencing a constant mental or physical disease.

Dysfunctional families do not recognize that issues exist. They do not discuss them or defy them. Thus, relatives figure out how to curb feelings and dismiss their own needs. They become "survivors." They create practices that help them deny, disregard, or maintain a strategic distance from difficult feelings. They separate themselves. They do not talk. They do not contact. They do not stand up to. They do not feel. They do not trust. The character and enthusiastic improvement of the individuals from a dysfunctional family are regularly repressed.

Consideration and vitality center around the relative who is sick or addicted. The mutually dependent individual ordinarily sacrifices their needs to deal with an individual who is wiped out. At the point when mutually dependent people place other individuals' wellbeing, welfare, and security before their own, they can lose contact with their very own needs, wants, and feelings of self.

How Do Co-dependent People Behave?

Mutually dependent people have low confidence and search for anything outside of themselves to make them feel good. They think that it is difficult to "act naturally." Some attempt to feel better through liquor, medications, or nicotine - and become addicted. Others may create habitual practices like workaholism, betting, or aimless sexual movement.

They mean well. They attempt to deal with an individual who is encountering difficulty, yet the caretaking ends up being intriguing. Mutually dependent people regularly take on a saint's job and become "supporters" to a person out of luck. A wife may cover for her alcoholic spouse; a mother may rationalize a truant tyke; or a dad may "pull a few strings" to shield his youngster from enduring the results of reprobate conduct.

The issue is that these rehashed salvage endeavors enable the penniless individual to proceed on a dangerous course and to turn out to be much progressively subject to the undesirable caretaking of the "supporter." As this dependence builds, the mutually dependent builds up a feeling of remuneration and fulfillment from "being required." When the caretaking ends up urgent, the mutually dependent feels choiceless and vulnerable in the relationship, however, it cannot split away from the cycle of conduct that causes it. Mutually dependent people see themselves as exploited people and are pulled in to that equivalent shortcoming in the affection and fellowship connections.

Qualities of Co-Dependent People are:

- A feeling of blame when championing themselves
- Lying/unscrupulousness
- Difficulty deciding
- An inclination to confound love and pity, with the propensity to "love" individuals they can pity and save
- An unfortunate reliance on connections. The mutually dependent will effectively clutch a relationship; to maintain a strategic distance from the sentiment of surrender
- Issues with closeness/limits
- An outrageous requirement for endorsement and acknowledgment
- A convincing need to control others
- Absence of trust in self and additionally others
- A misrepresented awareness of other's expectations for the activities of others
- The dread of being deserted or alone
- Difficulty identifying sentiments
- An inclination to wind up hurt when individuals do not perceive their endeavors
- Unbending nature/difficulty acclimating to change
- Incessant annoyance
- A propensity to accomplish more than their offer, constantly
- Poor correspondences

How Is Co-Dependency Treated?

Since codependency is typically established in an individual's adolescence, treatment regularly includes an investigation into early youth issues and their relationship to current ruinous personal conduct standards. Treatment incorporates instruction, experiential gatherings, and individual and gathering treatment through which mutually dependent people rediscover themselves and identify foolish standards of conduct. Treatment likewise centers around helping patients connect with sentiments that have been covered during adolescence and on reproducing relational peculiarities. The objective is to enable them to encounter their full scope of sentiments once more.

The initial phase in changing undesirable conduct is to get it. It is significant for mutually dependent people and their relatives to teach themselves about the course and cycle of addiction and how it stretches out into their connections. Libraries, medication, and liquor misuse treatment focus and psychological well-being focus frequently offer instructive materials and projects to people in general.

A great deal of progress and development is essential for mutually dependent and their family. Any caretaking conduct that permits or empowers maltreatment to proceed in the family should be perceived and halted. The mutually dependent must identify and grasp their sentiments and requirements. This may incorporate figuring out how to state "no," to cherish yet intense, and figuring out how to act naturally dependent. Individuals discover opportunity, love, and peacefulness in their recuperation.

Expectation lies in finding out additional. The more you comprehend codependency, the better you can adapt to its belongings. Connecting for information and help can enable somebody to carry on with a more beneficial, all the more satisfying life.

Codependency Tests

Codependency may mean somewhat different things to different individuals, yet basically, it is the point at which one individual is sacrificing more for their relationship than the other.

In sentimental connections, it is the point at which one partners needs over-the-top consideration and mental help, and frequently this is joined forces with them having a disease or an addiction which makes them considerably progressively reliant.

A codependent couple will not be beneficial for one another. For the most part, they will get together in light of the fact that either of them has a dysfunctional character, and as a rule, they will aggravate one another.

For instance, individuals engaged with narcissists will wind up giving and giving, yet it is rarely enough. Their partner will continue moving the goal lines and making unreasonable requests until the unfortunate casualty is totally worn out.

It is imperative to recollect that in a sound relationship, it is entirely expected to rely upon your partner for solace and backing. Be that as it may, there is a harmony between each partner's capacity to be autonomous and their capacity to appreciate common assistance, and if that parity is off, that is when things get muddled.

We approached different relationship specialists for the signs you could be in a codependent relationship. This is what they stated:

1. You need to 'fix' your partner

Everything begins as a fantasy, yet then your new partner begins to give a few indications of undesirable practices. Do you wind up making every one of the sacrifices to help your partner? Do you have an inclination that you lost yourself and you need the endorsement of your partner to be whole? Sound connections are made when the two partners have shared regard, trust, and are constantly fair with each other. Codependent characters will, in general, be accommodating people, blossoming from helping other people (or notwithstanding figuring they may 'fix' them). When thinking about someone else prevents you from having your very own needs met or if your self-esteem is reliant on being needed, you might head down the codependent way.

2. You have to request endorsement

If you believe you regularly need to get endorsement or authorization to do fundamental ordinary living, or if you believe you cannot settle on a basic choice without that individual, that could be an early indication of a codependent relationship. If you enter an association with heaps of certainty yet after some time, you start to question yourself, your self-esteem, and you are less definitive, you could be in a damaging narcissistic codependent relationship. If you have been constrained by your partner or they request being the essential chief in the relationship, at that point when you separate, you could even now accept and feel you need them.

It might be difficult to rationally isolate yourself from that perspective or even the routine of the relationship, yet when you can mend and better self-care, you can start to concentrate more on your needs and being a superior adaptation of yourself.

3. You lose contact with companions or family

I think when you start losing contact with the individuals who are imperative to you, it is a sign something is not exactly right. You start seeing that your essential center is the other individual, yet to the point where you are truly winding up very confined from individuals who were already significant. That being stated, I believe it is entirely ordinary when individuals begin to look all starry eyed at, for every other person to feel out of view. In any case, when it continues for some time, that is a noticeable sign you are getting to be unmoored from the grapples in your life that keep you consistent and keep you on the track which you have been on.

I think we should be extremely aware of that on the grounds that else we become progressively codependent on our partners, at that point, if you choose they aren't beneficial for you, you glance around and there are no companions, no leisure activities, and the world has turned into this one partner you have currently chosen is not right. In any case, presently leaving that partner, you are sacrificing the relationship, as well as life, since you have nothing else.

4. You are continually searching for consolation

How would you know if your relationship is codependent? Ask yourself these inquiries:

• Do both of you rationalize the other's awful or ill-bred conduct, or maintain a strategic distance from direct discussions about the condition of the relationship?

• Do you or your partner characterize yourselves by the relationship? Do you experience issues being separated from everyone else?

• Are you or your partner constantly stressed that the other will sever the relationship?

• Do you or your partner demonstration coquettishly with individuals outside of the relationship to make the different envious, or take steps to leave to make sure you can be asked to remain?

• Do both of you need consistent confirmation that you are cherished?

• Is there a ton of strain or power in your relationship, and do both of you subtly appreciate the 'show' of successive separations and reunions?

• Do you or your partner think of little tests to get consideration from the other?

5. You lose every one of your limits

One method for taking a gander at a codependent individual is if she is an over-provider. She generally feels excessively in charge of somebody or thinks about somebody. She truly feels like she needs to continue giving and giving, and overcompensating. These ladies can be extremely solid, yet the issue is they do not get a handle on the requirement for limits. Limits are entirely helpful with individuals you care about, yet in a codependent individual's heart, 'limits' is a grimy word. They think 'the minute I care about you, I drop every one of my limits. I let you ignore me since I trust you have a story, so I over-clarify away each and everything for you.' as such, you give more confidence to their story than to yours. You must have firm limits, since when you do not have them, or you are not mindful of them, you fall into the codependent trap.

6. You do not feel like you have your very own free life

In any relationship, it is imperative to both bond with your partner, yet in addition, keep up your very own life. You would prefer not to turn out to be so reliant on another person that you lose what your identity is, or that substance that makes you extraordinary. How would you keep up the two sides of yourself? Schedule date nights as well as evenings with companions or evenings alone to loosen up. At the start of a relationship, there is undeniable value in not going through consistently together and allowing yourselves to miss each other. Also, when you are getting things done alone, you become an all the more intriguing, balanced individual. In this way, a superior partner to anybody.

7. You start filling in the holes

The principal indication of codependency crawling into a relationship will include one individual beginning to assume on the liability to stay in contact and interface. As an partner pulls back in how much time, exertion, and care they are giving, the other partner intuitively fills in the hole by working harder to remain fortified. When this occurs, the relationship has shifted an undesirable way towards codependency.

8. Your partner has unfortunate propensities

One early indication of a codependent relationship (utilizing the primary meaning of an 'empowering agent') is the point at which one individual more than once takes part in an unfortunate conduct, for example, reliably drinking until they go out or pigging out until they feel wiped out, and the other individual either goes along with them in it, despite the fact that the individual doesn't really prefer to drink or voraciously consume food, or supports it for their own reasons.

If you addressed 'Yes' to even a couple of these inquiries, you are likely in a codependent relationship.

Chapter 2 – Revisiting Your Past

Dysfunctional Families

The expression "dysfunctional family," when utilized distinctly by experts, has turned out to be a prevalent language in America where dysfunctional families are the standard because of social qualities, a high separation rate, and broad addictions – from doctor-prescribed medications to working out, working, and shopping.

A sound family is a place of refuge – a position of sustenance and sustaining – that has a demeanor of receptiveness, immediacy, and liveliness, and takes into consideration the opportunity of articulation. There might be infrequent contentions and articulations of annoyance, yet harmony returns and people feel cherished and regarded. It works easily like a well-run organization. The officials – the guardians – make and concur upon principles, which are reliable and sensible.

Jack Welch, the previous CEO of General Electric, changed an organization that had a shut, internal-centered attitude, an inept administration, and uncommunicative workers. He understood the significance of making every representative feel like an esteemed member whose voice made a difference and prided himself on having an "open entryway" strategy that supported opportunity of articulation. Welch democratized the organization, giving a great many workers standard chances to challenge their managers and offer their thoughts in basic leadership. This strengthening style came about in flooded execution and representative fulfillment. They felt some portion of a group and that their voice made a difference. He despised mystery and refusal, and needed issues confronted and unraveled. He needed representatives that were free masterminds and candid about their thoughts and convictions, notwithstanding when awkward – when it "may sting." Employees were given direct input – positive and negative – and they thus assessed their managers. He sorted out discussions and critical thinking training. G.E. was a model of an open framework both all around. It looked worldwide for new thoughts from different organizations and shared the learning it picked up, which propelled its providers.

Obviously, a family doesn't have the capacity to boost generation and benefit, yet you can promptly observe that Welch's thoughts of transparency, direct correspondence, and populism increases worker's confidence, which occurs in sound families. In dysfunctional families, individuals have lower confidence and will, in general, be codependent. A portion of the side effects are depicted beneath, yet not all are important to make brokenness.

1. Unconventionality. Individuals have a sense of security when family life is unsurprising. If kids never recognize what state of mind Mom or Dad will be in, they cannot be unconstrained and are constantly on edge. Far more atrocious is mayhem, where the family is in a consistent emergency, frequently because of addiction, psychological sickness, or sexual, physical, or psychological mistreatment. Rather than a place of refuge, the family turns into a combat area to getaway. Kids may create substantial grievances, similar to cerebral pains and stomach hurts.

2. Assertion and Inconsistency. What are more regrettable than unbending standards are self-assertive and conflicting guidelines. Kids never know when they'll be rebuffed. Standards that do not bode well are unfair. This is merciless and breeds learned powerlessness and fierceness that can never be communicated. Youngsters are in steady dread, tread lightly, and feel miserable and angry on account of the capriciousness and injustice. Their feeling

of worth and nobility is disregarded. They lose regard and trust in their folks and specialist all in all. Since they're compelled to consent, some carry on with defiant or reprobate conduct, by doing ineffectively in school, or by utilizing drugs.

3. Privileged insights. A few insider facts are kept for ages about a family disgrace – regardless of whether addiction, savagery, crime, sexual issues, or psychological instability. The disgrace is felt by youngsters – notwithstanding when they do not have a clue about the mystery.

4. Powerlessness to Problem-Solve. Settling issues and clashes is vital to a smooth-running association. Be that as it may, in dysfunctional families, youngsters and guardians are accused more than once of something very similar and there are consistent contentions or quiet dividers of hatred. Nothing gets settled.

Conversely, solid families are protected in light of the fact that open self-articulation is energized without judgment or reprisal. Love is indicated in words, however in empathic, sustaining, and strong conduct. Every member, down to the youngest, is treated as an esteemed, regarded part. Input is permitted, and there is a feeling of uniformity, regardless of whether guardians have the last veto. Guardians act mindfully and are responsible for their responsibilities and consider kids responsible for theirs. They right and rebuff trouble making, however, do not accuse their kids or assault their character. Slip-ups are permitted and excused, and guardians recognize their very own inadequacies. They energize and direct their youngsters and regard their protection and physical and passionate limits. These fixings manufacture confidence, trust, and uprightness.

5. Dysfunctional Communication. This can take numerous structures – from the nonattendance of correspondence to verbal

maltreatment. Talking is not equivalent to utilitarian correspondence, which includes tuning in, regard, decisiveness, and comprehension. In dysfunctional families, correspondence is neither confident nor open. Individuals do not tune in and verbal maltreatment prevails. Kids are reluctant to express their contemplations and emotions, and are frequently accused, disgraced, or chastened for self-articulation. They are advised legitimately or in a roundabout way not to feel what they feel and might be named a sissy, terrible, idiotic, languid, or childish. They learn not to scrutinize their folks and not to confide their observations and emotions.

6. Refusal. Forswearing is an approach to overlook or imagine that an excruciating reality doesn't exist. Guardians attempt to act typical in the midst of family issues and emergencies, for example, a parent's nonappearance, sickness, or liquor addiction. It never gets discussed, nor the issue illuminated. This makes kids question their observations and communicates something specific that they cannot discuss something bizarre and startling – even to one another.

7. Unbending Rules. In certain families where there is physical or dysfunctional behavior, guardians are excessively remiss or unreliable, youngsters need direction and do not have a sense of security and pondering. By and large, be that as it may, there are prohibitive and subjective standards. Many are implicit. There is no space for mix-ups. A few guardians assume control over choices that kids should make and control their interests, school courses, companions, and dress. Normal autonomy is viewed as traitorousness and deserting. They forbid discussing things regarded unseemly, for example, sex, passing, the holocaust, grandpa's limp, or that father was hitched previously. A few families have guidelines limiting the declaration of resentment, abundance, or crying. At the point when sentiments cannot be communicated,

youngsters learn restraint and become excessively controlled or controlling grown-ups, all adding to low-confidence.

8. Job Confusion. This happens when a parent is sincerely or physically missing or is unreliable and a kid takes on parental duties or turns into a buddy or compatriot to the next parent. This is habitually the situation after a separation, yet additionally occurs in unblemished families where guardians need closeness. This is age-improper and harming the kid mentally, who should now act like somewhat grown-up, subdue their needs and sentiments, and may feel that the individual is deceiving the other parent.

9. A Closed System. A shut family will not permit differing or new plans to be talked about among individuals or with strangers. Individuals aren't permitted to discuss the family to other people, and probably will not permit visitors from another race or religion. A few families are secluded and do not communicate with society. Others do, yet appearances are everything, and reality with regards to the family is not shared. At base are fears of unique thoughts and disgrace.

Today, organizations, youthful families, and countries are ending up increasingly open and populist – a confident sign for what's to come.

Addiction

Codependency is a condition where people endeavor and accept that if they control individuals, spots, and circumstances, they can infer a feeling of self-esteem. It takes after an addiction to dealing with the requirements and the issues of someone else. Truth be told, a considerable lot of the individuals I've worked with who are in these kinds of codependent connections end up inclination, by and large, what can be depicted as exemplary indications of addiction. A portion of the encounters they report include:

- Lifestyle changes
- On edge or neurotic intuition with no undeniable reason
- Changes as a part of their character as announced by loved ones
- Absence of inspiration or dormancy

In the wake of decision out that an individual is manhandling substances, for example, liquor or medicates, and discovering that their side effects are not indications of other enthusiastic or psychological well-being issues, I find what they are encountering is, truth be told, constant, dynamic, and backsliding addiction. In actuality, many who are in codependent connections basically turned out to be reliant on the individuals with whom they are seeing someone.

Negative feelings

In that capacity, many think that it is difficult to "quit" the relationship, much like an individual addicted to liquor experiences issues stopping drinking. The "relationship addiction" controls an individual's capacity to justify and settle on solid choices to their best advantage. Their lives end up being affected in a negative way because they are too reliant on another person for emotional support.

Four Key Strides to Codependency Recuperation

Finding a specialist who makes you feel good and safe is an incredible spot to start for any individual who wishes to change codependency problems. When getting past codependency problems, consider the following:

Creating information of what a sound relationship resembles: I never expect that an individual admitting and tolerating the addiction part of codependency requires some serious energy, and since it is a backsliding condition, urging individuals to keep on chipping away at their recuperation each day, in turn, is basic to their prosperity and possible mending. Experiencing codependency has a decent comprehension of what a solid relationship resembles. An aspect of my responsibilities is helping individuals comprehend what's in store in a sound relationship.

Codependency recuperation is a procedure: Many people who experience it have been rehearsing dysfunctional relationship aptitudes for the greater part of their lives. Conceding and tolerating the addiction segment of codependency requires some investment, and since it is a backsliding condition, urging individuals to keep on taking a shot at their recuperation each day is basic to their prosperity and possible mending.

Building up a sound feeling of self-identify: Like numerous individuals living with addiction, numerous individuals who are codependent battle with what their identity is and what their motivation is. Once in a while, they are mindful and sensitive to their internal identity talk, and every now and then, have no clue what they like or do not care for.

Limit building: One of the most significant strides to ace in the voyage of codependency recuperation is figuring out how to construct proper enthusiastic limits. Helping the individual with codependency in discovering that the person in question doesn't have control over others is a critical advance in creating solid connections.

Learning self-approval: People with codependency regularly have a dubious meaning of self, so directing an individual to figure out how to endure awkward sentiments, let go of pointless examples of conduct, and practice self-approval will help during the time spent structure confidence.

Codependency has been alluded to as "relationship addiction" or "love addiction." The emphasis on others lightens our torment and internal void, however, in disregarding ourselves, it just develops. This propensity turns into a round, self-sustaining framework that takes on its very own life. Our reasoning winds up over the top, and our conduct can be habitual, notwithstanding unfavorable outcomes. Models may call an partner or ex we realize we shouldn't, putting ourselves or qualities in danger to suit somebody, or snooping out of desire or dread. This is the reason codependency has been alluded to as an addiction. In 1956, it chose that addiction was a sickness, and in 2013, additionally named heftiness a malady. A prime inspiration in the two cases was to de-deride these conditions and empower treatment.

Is Codependency a Disease?

In 1988, therapists recommended that codependency is an illness taking note of the addictive procedure. A therapist and specialist of interior medication, Charles Whitfield, portrayed codependence as an interminable and dynamic ailment of "lost-selfhood" with unmistakable, treatable side effects — simply like substance reliance.

Codependency is additionally portrayed by manifestations that shift on a continuum like those related to chronic drug use. They go from gentle to serious and incorporate reliance, forswearing, dysfunctional passionate reactions, longing for and remunerate (through connection with someone else), and failure to control or swear off urgent conduct without treatment. You progressively invest energy contemplating, being with, and additionally attempting to control someone else, similarly as a medication junkie with a medication. Other social, recreational, or work exercises endure accordingly. At long last, you may proceed with your conduct as well as the relationship, in spite of relentless or repeating social or relational issues it makes.

Phases of Codependency

Codependency is constant with suffering side effects that are additionally dynamic, implying that they intensify after some time without intercession and treatment. As I would see it, codependency starts in youth because of a dysfunctional family condition. In any case, youngsters are normally reliant; it cannot be analyzed until adulthood, and for the most part, starts to manifest in cozy connections. There are three identifiable stages prompting expanding reliance on the individual or relationship and comparing loss of self-center and self-care.

Beginning period

The beginning period may resemble any sentimental association with expanded consideration and reliance on your partner and want to satisfy the person in question. Be that as it may, with codependency, we can wind up fixated on the individual, deny or defend risky conduct, question our discernments, neglect to keep up sound limits and surrender our own companions and exercises.

Center Stage

Bit by bit, there is expanded exertion required to limit excruciating parts of the relationship, and uneasiness, blame, and self-accuse set in. After some time, our confidence decreases as we bargain a greater amount of ourselves to keep up the relationship. Outrage, dissatisfaction, and hatred develop. Then we empower or attempt to change our partner through consistence, control, annoying, or accusing. We may conceal issues and pull back from family and companions. There might possibly be misuse or brutality, however, our state of mind declines, and fixation, reliance, and struggle, withdrawal, or consistence increases. We may utilize other addictive practices to adapt, for example, eating less junk food, shopping, working, or mishandling substances.

Late Stage

Presently, the enthusiastic and social side effects start to influence our wellbeing. We may experience pressure-related issues, for example, stomach related and rest issues, migraines, muscle strain or agony, dietary issues, TMJ, sensitivities, sciatica, and coronary illness. Over the top impulsive conduct or different addictions increment, just as the absence of confidence and self-care. Sentiments of sadness, outrage, gloom, and misery develop.

Recuperation

Fortunately, the indications are reversible when a codependent enters treatment. Individuals do not look for assistance until there is an emergency or they're in enough agony to persuade them. Ordinarily, they aren't mindful of their codependency and may likewise be willfully ignorant about another person's maltreatment as well as addiction. Recovery starts with instruction and leaving refusal. Finding out about codependency is a decent start, yet more prominent change happens through treatment and going to a Twelve-Step program.

In recuperation, you increase trust and the center shifts from the other individual to yourself. There are early, middle, and late phases of recuperation that parallel recuperation from different addictions. In the center stage, you start to manufacture your very own character, confidence, and the capacity to decisively express sentiments, needs, and needs. You learn self-obligation, limits, and self-care. Psychotherapy frequently incorporates mending PTSD and youth injury.

In the late stage, joy and confidence don't rely upon others. You gain the limit with regard to both self-sufficiency and closeness. You experience your own capacity and self-esteem. You feel broad and innovative, with the capacity to produce and seek after your own objectives.

Codependency doesn't consequently vanish when an individual leaves a codependent relationship. Recuperation requires progressing support, and there is no ideal restraint. In any case, codependent conduct can, without much of a stretch, return under expanded pressure or if you go into a dysfunctional relationship. Hairsplitting is a side effect of codependency. There is nothing of the sort as immaculate recuperation. Repeating side effects simply present continuous learning openings.

Abuse

Connections between individuals are solid when they are interconnected. In an interconnected relationship, every individual has their very own needs addressed and endeavors to address the issues of the other individual. An issue happens, nonetheless, when connections are interconnected, yet are codependent.

In codependent connections, the requirements of one individual being filled by the other are undesirable or improper. One of the most well-known situations of codependency is a heavy drinker who is routinely provided with alcohol by the other individual in the relationship, despite the fact that the alcoholic can turn out to be verbally or physically oppressive when inebriated. The inquiry at that point moves toward becoming, "For what reason would that individual oblige and even help such conduct?" The appropriate response is codependency, and frequently, the reason is psychological mistreatment.

The genuinely manhandled end up in codependent connections in light of a craving to be required, regardless of whether the need is to give the following beverage. Also, despite the fact that a relationship is codependent, in any event, it is needy in some sense. Psychological mistreatment frequently scars the victim. They feel dishonorable to be adored, all by themselves. In a codependent relationship, their value is effectively characterized. They are regularly advised that they are so critical to that individual, particularly when they are giving what that individual needs. To feel esteem, even dependent on unseemly or destructive conduct, the individual who has been genuinely manhandled will go into or proceed in an unfortunate codependent relationship.

The psychological mistreatment succeeds when the abuser can supplant your own authority over yourself with their control. You never again confide in yourself, yet rather enable the abuser to hold undue impact over your considerations and activities. The abuser progresses toward becoming, generally, a piece of you, controlling you and how you see yourself and your reality. The limit between where you start and the abuser closures is obscured.

In resulting connections, you may end up totally surrendering to the next individual, thoroughly submerging yourself in the other individual's character, tolerating their perspective on the world and of you. Lamentably, you may look for somebody who is predominant and controlling with whom to set up a relationship. The jobs in this new relationship will fit into an anticipated example.

Then again, you might be incredibly touchy to anything you think appears to be remotely similar to control. It might be difficult for you to keep up cozy connections, on the grounds that to have closeness may trigger an exceptionally delicate reaction on your part. Also, you might be exceptionally suspicious of any individual who tries to become acquainted with you in a profound, individual manner. You may set up boundaries to keep individuals out.

At long last, there is simply the peril of ending up very retained. If your experience has consistently been that whatever you did or didn't do brought a quick, extraordinary response, you may have reasoned that the world truly did, in actuality, spin around you. You may have built up a propensity for dissecting everything that occurs around you as it identifies with you.

While these strategies helped you endure your maltreatment, they have left you not well arranged to work inside solid, positive connections. Endeavoring to submerge yourself totally into a solid relationship may make you seem possessive and tenacious or choking to the next individual. Then again, a doubt of closeness and a general standoffish quality may prevent most others from endeavoring an association with you. What's more, being amazingly self-retained practically rules out contemplations of others.

If you do not have a clue what a codependent relationship is, it is when two individuals in a relationship give up their freedom and build up an undesirable reliance on one another. In this, one partner is so fixated on the requirements of the other that they overlook their very own needs. Therefore, the other partner controls the relationship in an egotistical and regularly injurious way.

This is a perilous dynamic, yet it is not as simple to identify as you may suspect. While codependent connections may have physical maltreatment, all have enthusiastic and mental maltreatment. This kind of maltreatment is regularly very difficult to identify. It gradually crawls into the relationship and turns into an example of conduct that the codependent cannot change.

The causes of psychological mistreatment in a relationship can begin all of a sudden, or they can build slowly. Regularly, what's seen by the codependent partner as cherishing and mindful partner is really a controller, a stalker, and an individual who is separating and nourishing off the requirements of the codependent.

The Effects and Impact of Emotional, Mental, and Verbal Abuse

The different traits we all have affect the people around us in different ways an it is important to understand the impact they have on relationships.

Since codependents dread being separated from everyone else and get such a large amount of their identity from their association with their partner, they have issues saying no or defending themselves when they start to experience misuse. Saying no frequently brings about progressively verbal maltreatment, seclusion, and dangers to leave—all issues that are actually what the codependent is attempting to keep away from.

This creates a situation where the narcisstic iniviual takes avantage of the one who is codependent and they are unable to do without each other.

It is critical to understand that, much the same as physical maltreatment, the enthusiastic, mental, and verbal maltreatment is purposeful behavior by the abuser. The narcissist utilizes this conduct to get what they need, purposefully tearing down the other individual's confidence, self-esteem, and capacity to support themselves.

Perceiving Gaslighting

Another regular type of passionate and verbal maltreatment is gaslighting. This is definitely not another conduct, however it is as of late been identified and named as a conduct utilized by the individuals who take part in psychological mistreatment.

Gaslighting is, here and there, more difficult to distinguish and more harming than some different sorts of psychological mistreatment. In this kind of maltreatment, the abuser controls the codependent by giving false data or false memories that reason the codependent to start to scrutinize their rational soundness and their capacity to review and recall things effectively.

At times, gaslighting is the utilization of refusals that things happened. This is not just differences in memory. It is malignant, purposeful, and intended to make blame, vulnerability, and uncertainty in your brain.

There are some regular signs that gaslighting is going on the relationship. To help identify this conduct, search for the accompanying:

Giving false data: To justify a lie, an abuser giving false information will discuss other individuals. For instance, a man may tell a lady she was playing with somebody at a gathering, and everybody saw and was discussing it. He may make articulations about what others said and how they saw the conduct.

Concealing conduct: If an partner is trapped in a falsehood, frequently they will utilize misleads endeavor to clarify away the issue. In any case, the untruths are rehashed again and again, and might be clearly incorrect records of what has happened. Simultaneously, the codependent is probably not going to challenge the untruth, and it continues getting rehashed until it is hard for the codependent to review the specifics of the circumstance.

As gaslighting can be difficult to recognize, conversing with an advisor and building a solid encouraging group of people will be basic to evade further harm to your confidence.

Illnesses

One of the most testing parts of life is shaping sound bonds and associations with others. Frequently now and again, an individual who has encountered injury shapes an undesirable faithfulness to others. This implies that the unfortunate casualties have a specific dysfunctional connections that happen within the sight of peril, disgrace, or misuse.

In these connections, an individual may encounter more mishandle, self-damage, fixation, doubt, and other negative outcomes of the bond. Another, and normal, aftereffect of addiction and harsh conditions, is codependency. Codependency alludes to a kind of dysfunctional relationship where one individual empowers someone else's addiction, poor emotional well-being, adolescence, untrustworthiness, or under-accomplishment.

Co-dependency can be a difficult issue to work with in treatment since it can turn into an unrecognizable addiction. Frequently, one winds up over the top with the relationship and bond they shaped with another that it is regularly not seen that their bond is undesirable. An individual cannot control their bond with someone else paying little heed to the treachery, decimation, or misuse. The individual who has co-dependency problem is increasingly centered around the abuser. So as to mend and discover injury goals, an individual must be capable and willing to perceive how their habitual conduct just guides in shaping injury bonds and in this way they should break the compulsivity.

Codependency then again, concentrates more on the addiction. Injury holding and codependency possibly meet up when the someone who is addicted is likewise an oppressive culprit. The individual who will in general be codependent likely was engaged with some type of addiction through relatives, companions, and so on. Along these lines, the individual is activated by other people who have addiction. Codependency is additionally not "terrifying" yet increasingly about thinking about others needs rather than their own. In treating codependency, it is significant for the individual to be increasingly mindful of one's self, reasonability, and permitting care into their lives from themselves.

In treating others, it is essential to perceive the difference between injury holding and codependency. Shaping relationship are difficult in their very own right, yet when including injury, treachery, stress, addiction, misuse, and absence of self-care, connections can turn out to be very unfortunate and there is a requirement for intercessions. Both injury holding and codependency can cause extreme outcomes. It is imperative to enable the individual to identify whether a relationship has turned out to be addictive or whether they should disengage affectionately and care for themselves. Frequently this can be accomplished by dismembering associations with a specialist and figuring out how to define fitting limits and give up. Since with the give up and acknowledgment of how to break the undesirable bonds, an individual builds up their actual feeling of self and capacity to make dependable and solid connections.

"In a war, warriors are compelled to deny their feelings so as to endure. This enthusiastic disavowal attempts to enable the warrior to endure the war, yet later can have obliterating postponed results. The restorative calling has now perceived the injury and harm that this enthusiastic refusal can cause, and have instituted a term to depict the impacts of this sort of forswearing. That term is "Postponed Stress Syndrome."

In a war fighters need to deny what it feels like to see companions executed and debilitated; what it feels like to murder other individuals and make them endeavor to slaughter you. There is injury brought about by the occasions themselves. There is injury because of the need of preventing the enthusiastic effect from claiming the occasions. There is injury from the impacts the passionate refusal has on the individual's life after he/she has come back from the war in light of the fact that as long is the individual is denying his/her enthusiastic injury she/he is precluding a section from claiming her/himself.

The pressure brought about by the injury, and the impact of denying the injury, by denying self, in the end surfaces in manners which produce new injury - nervousness, liquor and medication misuse, bad dreams, wild rage, failure to look after connections, powerlessness to hold employments, suicide, and so forth.

Codependence is a type of Delayed Stress Syndrome.

Rather than blood and demise (albeit some experience blood and passing actually), what befell us as youngsters was otherworldly demise and enthusiastic harming, mental torment and physical infringement. We had to grow up preventing the truth from securing what was going on in our homes. We had to deny our sentiments about what we were encountering and seeing and detecting. We had to deny our selves.

We grew up denying the enthusiastic reality: of parental liquor abuse, addiction, dysfunctional behavior, rage, viciousness, misery, surrender, double-crossing, hardship, disregard, inbreeding, and so on and so on.; of our folks battling or the fundamental pressure and outrage since they weren't being straightforward enough to battle; of father's overlooking us due to his workaholism as well as mother covering us since she had no other personality than being a mother; of the maltreatment that one parent stacked on another who wouldn't safeguard him/herself and additionally the maltreatment we got from one of our folks while the other wouldn't shield us; of having just one parent or of having two guardians who remained together and shouldn't have; and so forth., and so forth.

We grew up with messages like: kids ought to be seen and not heard; huge young men do not cry and little women do not blow up; it is not alright to resent somebody you adore - particularly your folks; god cherishes you however will send you to consume in hellfire always if you contact your dishonorable private parts; do not make commotion or run or in any capacity be a typical youngster; do not commit errors or do anything incorrectly; and so on., and so forth.

We were naturally introduced to the center of a war where our feeling of self was battered and cracked and broken into pieces. We experienced childhood in war zones where our creatures were limited, our discernments refuted, and our sentiments overlooked and nullified.

The war we were naturally introduced to, the front line every one of us experienced childhood in, was not in some outside nation against some identified "foe" - it was in the "homes" which should be our place of refuge with our folks whom we Loved and trusted to deal with us. It was not for a year or a few - it was for sixteen or seventeen or eighteen years.

We encountered what is classified "asylum injury" - our most secure spot to be was not protected - and we encountered it once a day for quite a long time and years. The absolute most noteworthy harm was done to us in inconspicuous ways regularly on the grounds that our haven was a war zone.

It was anything but a front line in light of the fact that our folks weren't right or awful - it was a war zone since they were at war inside, on the grounds that they were naturally introduced to the center of a war. By doing our mending we are turning into the sincerely legit good examples that our folks never got the opportunity to be. Through being in Recovery we are breaking the cycles of foolish conduct that have managed human presence for a huge number of years.

Codependence is an awful and amazing type of Delayed Stress Syndrome. The injury of feeling like we were not protected in our very own homes makes it exceptionally difficult to feel like we are sheltered anyplace. Having an inclination that we were not adorable to our very own folks makes it difficult to accept that anybody can Love us.

Codependence is being at war with ourselves - which makes it difficult to trust and Love ourselves. Codependence is precluding parts from claiming ourselves so we do not have the foggiest idea what our identity is.

Recuperation from the malady of Codependence includes halting the war inside so we can connect with our True Self, so we can begin to Love and confide in ourselves."

Chapter 3 – The Recovery Process

Setting Boundaries

In sentimental connections we frequently consider limits an awful thing or basically superfluous. Is not our partner expected to foresee our wants and needs? Is not that piece of being infatuated? Aren't limits unfeeling? Do not they meddle with the sentiment and immediacy of a relationship?

Every solid relationship have limits. A limit is "where I end and another person starts." Boundaries seeing someone are compared to the limits around states.

With no line the differentiation ends up confounding: Who possesses and keeps up this questionable space? Which guidelines apply?

At the point when the limit is obviously characterized and regarded, you needn't bother with dividers or electric wall, Individuals can even cross the limit every so often when there is a shared comprehension. Be that as it may, when the limit is damaged so as to do mischief or exploit, at that point you'll likely need dividers, doors and watchmen.

In sound connections partners ask consent, consider each other's emotions, show appreciation and regard differences in conclusion, point of view and sentiments.

In less sound connections, partners expect their partner feels a similar way they do. They overlook the impacts of disregarding their partner's limit (e.g., "They'll get over it").

Limits in sentimental connections are particularly basic, on the grounds that instead of different connections, partners possess each other's most private spaces, including physical, enthusiastic and sexual, he said.

This is the reason imparting your limits obviously is vital. Be that as it may, what does — and doesn't — this resemble?

Beneath, you'll discover bits of knowledge on limits that do not work and tips for defining limits that do.

Limits that Do not Work

Limits that frequently fizzle are those that incorporate the words 'consistently,' 'never' or any supreme language. Such limits are normally unreasonable and do not last.

Other poor limits estrange you from your partner, have a twofold standard or attempt to control a result. If you aren't home by 8 p.m. consistently, I will not engage in sexual relations with you," "If you do not do X, I will hurt myself" or "You are not permitted to do X, yet I can do it when I please."

Obscure limits additionally do not work. These incorporate "Do not spend a great deal of cash this month" or "Get the children from school a couple of times each week."

Numerous partners do not discuss their limits. They anticipate that their partner should simply know them. This is out of line. For example, you need your partner to perceive your achievements. Rather than communicating this need, you indicate it, play a round of "I'll luxuriously confirm you if you'll furnish a proportional payback" or sulk around when it doesn't occur.

In addition to the fact that this is incapable, it makes disarray and can hurt your relationship.

Defining Healthy Limits

As per analyst Leslie Becker-Phelps, Ph.D, sound limits incorporate everything from making some noise when you believe you are being disregarded to supporting for yourself to possess energy for your own advantages.

Attempt the sandwich approach. This comprises of a compliment, analysis, compliment. Beginning with a compliment keeps your partner from getting protective. "This primes them for a little analysis, they feel associated and agreeable enough to take it, and after that it closes with a compliment."

Model: "I cherish engaging in sexual relations with you, it is a mind blowing some portion of our relationship. I find that I'm for the most part in the state of mind in the first part of the prior day work, and around evening time I simply need to rest. Would we be able to continue having the best sex ever in the mornings?"

Be clear about your needs. After you realize what your needs are, tell your partner. Numerous limit infringement come from errors. One partner has an issue with specific practices, yet they never let their partner know. Regularly this is on the grounds that they stress it'll trigger a contention.

Be that as it may, it is OK to have inclinations, and it is OK to tell your darling. For example, if you need to be treated as an equivalent with budgetary issues, tell your partner.

Be specific and direct. As indicated by Levy, the more specific you are with imparting your limit, the better. She shared these models:

"If you put your messy garments in the hamper by 10 a.m. on Saturday morning, I'll be glad to wash them for you."

"Try not to peruse my diary. I feel damaged when my security is slighted."

"I need to catch wind of your day. I'll be accessible to give you my complete consideration in 10 minutes."

Be clear about your adoration, while being clear about your limits. Convey to your partner the amount you care about them. If they've exceeded a limit, notice this. "State that you need them to regard the limit, and clarify the significance of this to you."

"I cherish you however am not willing to phone in wiped out for you when you have been drinking."

She shared this model: "I need you to realize that I cherish you and have each goal of us working through whatever issues come up. In any case, I disapprove of you being verbally harsh when you blow up. If you need to discuss how it upset you that I kept running into my former sweetheart, we can do that, yet just if you do not assault me."

Becker-Phelps additionally recommended staying open to hearing how the limit influences your partner. Talk through the issue so both of you feel regarded, heard and thought about, she said.

Use "I" proclamations. As per Levy, "I" explanations "help you claim your own sentiments and enable your partner to feel more quiet and less protective." Rather than saying, "You have to do this," or "You ought to consistently," utilize such expresses as: "I feel," or "I would acknowledge," or "I might want it if... "

Act naturally mindful. The initial phase in defining any limit is self-information. You have to recognize what you like and aversion, what you are OK with versus what panics you, and how you need to be treated in given circumstances.

While there is no assurance this will consistently work, individuals will in general be progressively responsive to analysis when they first feel heard and comprehended.

At last, sound connections require obvious parameters. For example, most couples concur that deceiving is a limit infringement. Yet, I do not get cheating's meaning? Is it physical contact, going to lunch, imparting insider facts to a partner, fantasizing about somebody or watching pornography?

At the point when couples are clear about the limits for their own relationship, what the principles, objectives, and desires are, the relationship can be steady.

Putting Yourself First

Self-Care

Declining to deal with yourself doesn't make you a saint deserving of awards yet rather presumably an all out torment to live with. This may sound nonsensical however bodes well if you think about that we as a whole need the ones we want to be glad, solid, and around for whatever length of time that conceivable. You may stress your partner by not dealing with your wellbeing since this may mean losing you to a preventable ailment.

Comparative principles apply when you do not deal with your enthusiastic wellbeing. Perhaps you are discouraged or constantly troubled at work yet will not change employments or get help through treatment. You may feel qualified for your partner's compassion consistently and that is consistent with some degree. Life can be tireless and periodically gives us a crude arrangement yet when your misery ends up incessant and you stay aloof about fixing the issue, requesting proceeded with compassion transforms into a childish demonstration. No one needs to return home to wretchedness consistently.

Besides, it is extremely excruciating to see our friends and family endure so you are by all account not the only one in torment when you are troubled. In truth, none of us can provide for others what we cannot provide for ourselves so our ability to deal with ourselves and satisfy ourselves is firmly attached to our capacity to provide for others liberally. Both of you merit a significant other who assumes liability for their wellbeing and satisfaction.

In this way, despite the fact that you may feel pulled in various ways by the entirety of your obligations, set aside a few minutes consistently for these fundamental strides of self-care:

Look for approaches to develop and figure out how to remain occupied with life.

This could be perusing another creator or building up another diversion. When we are youthful, everything provokes our interest and feels new and energizing yet as we get more seasoned, it is anything but difficult to simply stay with a similar old, same old. Try not to exhaust and unsurprising however rather observe something new to be energized and converse with your partner about.

Eat well, get enough rest, and exercise routinely.

Life is short and you just get one body to live it with so treat it like the essential need it is. Utilize sound judgment and deal with it consistently in little ways and enormous.

Invest quality energy as a team.

Shut occasions out each week where you do not participate in pressure talk about work, bills, and so on. Rather, see a motion picture together or plan an excursion to the recreation center or exhibition hall. During those occasions, turn off your PDA. Regardless of whether it is a full night out or simply making up for lost time in the first part of the day or night, having even only 30 minutes of together time can help with fashioning a more grounded bond. Feeling near others is nature's Prozac without the expenses and symptoms so use it liberally.

Invest energy with loved ones.

We are social creatures and nothing feeds us like our connections. Offering a chuckle to friends and family makes our ordinary stresses fall away and interfaces us to something greater. This experience is pivotal for our prosperity since it assuages pressure.

Dealing with yourself physically and genuinely makes you progressively present, centered, and quiet. Be the individual that you would need to get back home to, somebody who chips away at their own prosperity and satisfaction and hence has the transmission capacity to make another person cheerful as well.

To wrap things up, if you feel that your partner is not rehearsing self-care, make some noise and converse with them about it. Call attention to why it makes a difference to you and how it influences your relationship. Be strong and energetic about it as much as you can and offer recommendations. Ideally, your partner will be available to your endeavors to improve the nature of the relationship. If the individual in question is not, you can generally attempt couple's treatment to improve correspondence.

Mindfulness and Meditation

Care is a frame of mind to living that encourages you be progressively open, caring, and mindful. It includes purposely coordinating your consideration away from autopilot and negative, making a decision about musings, enabling you to be progressively present and associated with whatever is going on this moment. It is anything but a major stretch to envision that increasingly careful individuals may improve relationship partners. Furthermore, presently there is clear research support for this relationship. A meta-investigation distributed in the Journal of Human Sciences and Extension a year ago found that more elevated amounts of care anticipate more joyful, all the more fulfilling connections.

Does care really cause relationship upgrades?

Before we go any further, it is critical to take note of that of the 10 investigations that were incorporated, just two contained a care mediation. The others simply estimated care and relationship fulfillment and found a positive connection between them (correlational investigations). This raises the chicken and egg issue. Do more joyful connections make us feel increasingly present and open, as opposed to the a different way? In spite of the fact that we do not know without a doubt that care produces relationship improvement, in any event two investigations demonstrate that it does. In any case, why? The appropriate response may lie in how care influences the cerebrum.

The following are five cerebrum based manners by which rehearsing care may enable you to have more joyful connections:

1. Care improves feeling guideline

Studies demonstrate that care practice fortifies the prefrontal cortex and improves the availability between the prefrontal cortex and amygdala. The prefrontal cortex is the cerebrum's official focus and it can make an impression on the amygdala revealing to it that things are alright and it can chill and stop the "battle, flight, solidify" reaction. So notwithstanding when we do begin to lose it or leave our partners when they are highly involved with talking, we can say "Stop! This is not useful" and in this way prevent ourselves from going down a relationship bunny opening.

2. Care encourages us be progressively present and mindful

The vast majority of us realize how disappointing it tends to be to attempt to converse with an partner who is continually checking email or messages or whose consideration is consistently on work stresses. Care changes territories of the cerebrum related with coordinating consideration and core interest. In this manner, care can enable us to see when we are on autopilot and divert thoughtfulness regarding whatever our partner is stating or to what they might feel and requiring. This can enable us to be additionally cherishing and present in our connections, which assembles closeness and makes our connections more joyful and progressively associated.

3. Care makes us increasingly empathic

Care additionally changes the insula, a piece of the mind related with sympathy and empathy. This can enable us to be all the more comprehension of our partners' viewpoints and feelings and feel more sympathy for them. When we approach our partners sympathetically, as opposed to with resentment and want to control them, this can take the discussion a positive way. Sympathy additionally encourages us express love and warmth to our partner, which manufactures closeness. Care makes a methodology, as opposed to an evasion attitude.

4. Care upgrades mindfulness

Care likewise prompts changes in the foremost cingulate cortex, which is related with our feeling of self and feeling guideline. In this way care may enable us to see when we are carrying on in undesirable ways and divert consideration back to how we'd like to act and what our guiding principle are. This can enable us to control the motivation to act dangerously or manipulatively. It might enable you to get up and accomplish something different when you are enticed to break into your partner's PC or stalk them on the web.

5. Care brings down negative enthusiastic reactivity

Care studies demonstrate that rehearsing care for 8 to 10 weeks changes the cerebrum's feeling guideline regions. The amygdala is a little, almond-molded piece of the midbrain that captures the cerebrum into "battle, flight, solidify" mode in which we begin to consider our to be as dangers to our prosperity or self-sufficiency and naturally shut down sincerely or begin to assault them with furious words and deeds. Care contracts the volume of the amygdala, implying that it has less capacity to capture us into 'danger" mode. This can help couples escape negative cycles of damaging contending or passionate removing.

We as a whole need more joyful connections however few of us know the keys to relationship fulfillment. Instead of concentrating vitality on grumbling or attempting to change your partner, take up a care practice. Far and away superior, take a care course together or practice reflection utilizing a care application. This will enable you to be progressively present, cherishing, and sincerely develop. What's more, who can oppose that?

Let Your Emotions Out

Peculiar things happen when we get injured. Hurt is a tragic inclination; subsequently, it bodes well that we would react in misery when a life partner or relative (irregular models, I guarantee you) offends us. Be that as it may, rather than crying about our torment in such cases, we are undeniably bound to lash out in fierceness! Go figure.

Things being what they are, our response is reasonable. Outrage has two variations: essential displeasure and optional indignation. Essential annoyance happens when a limit has been crossed. Infringement sign fury as a safeguard system so as to prepare a viable reaction. For example, if we happen to observe Anger has two variations; a harasser strolling by our sweet young lady and pulls hard on her hair, our moment fury will enable us to make fast move to address the circumstance. Something very similar happens when our own limits are disregarded in child rearing: Picture a youngster not tuning in to his parent. Everything inside the parent says this situation is not right, and fury regularly ascends to the surface ("you have to tune in to your folks, youthful man!"). In this circumstance, be that as it may, we have to kill the annoyance flag and chill off a piece so as to think of the best and suitable child rearing arrangement.

Optional annoyance—brutal as it in some cases may be—is, at its center, a passionate injury instead of a sign. Here and there called "receptive outrage," it is an enthusiastic reaction as opposed to an unadulterated feeling. The unadulterated feeling is harmed. At the point when an individual feels hurt, the person may react with indignation. It is actually the same than if the individual reacted by hitting the sack. In the previous case (when an individual gets distraught), the reaction is enthusiastic in nature; in the last case (when the individual hits the hay), the reaction is social in nature.

In the two cases, the genuine inclination being experienced is harmed.

We should picture a spouse saying something harmful to his wife (once more, you may need to consider something you read some place . . .). When the words leave his mouth, she feels a cut in her heart. It is instinctive. It harms.

Wife: "I have a good thought! For what reason do not we take a family excursion? The children would love it!"

Spouse: "Do you ever think before you open your mouth?"

Presently, I realize you may ask why the spouse would state a wonder such as this, yet remember marriage is perplexing, and couple of things are what they appear from the start to be. For this situation, for example, this couple has been talking about the spouse's agonizing money related worry for half a month in their conjugal directing. He has communicated his dread of getting a cardiovascular failure from all the weight he feels. With the instructor's assistance, they have gone to an understanding that the wife will, throughout the following couple of months, abstain from requesting that the spouse burn through cash on any "additional items" for the family. Without It is instinctive. It harms. Thinking, be that as it may, the wife currently energetically raises the possibility of a family excursion, which will of need include some cost. Subsequently the spouse's burning answer.

Her very own conduct in any case, the wife reels in torment. "How might he converse with me like that?" she ponders. She feels rejected, squashed, abused and extremely, hurt. So she opens her mouth and starts screaming at her better half. "How could YOU SPEAK TO ME LIKE THAT? DO YOU EVER THINK BEFORE OPENING

YOUR MOUTH? YOU ARE MEAN, DISGUSTING, DESPICABLE . . ."
That is optional outrage.

Our sages disclose to us that outrage is a hazardous inclination. Outrage can cause enormous profound mischief, just as passionate, mental and physical damage. It prompts numerous wrongdoings, including the offenses of harming individuals with words, treating individuals forcefully, utilizing foul language, and numerous others. Optional annoyance is the most perilous sort of all since, sitting as it does on an open injury, one is probably going to lash out with the full power of the enthusiastic agony that releases it. Words once verbally expressed cannot be withdrawn. Who knows what number of broken relationships are the aftereffect of hearts broken by reactionary verbal maltreatment?

So as to maintain a strategic distance from the statement of reactionary resentment, we should prepare ourselves to keep our mouths solidly shut at whatever point we feels aches of hurt. It offers a reward "more brilliant than the sun" to the individuals who can ace this aptitude. That reward will occur on the planet to come, however there are additionally remunerates that happen directly here, in this world. With our mouths shut, our talking device cannot turn into an instrument of the underhanded tendency. We are spared from profound mischief. Also, our most significant connections are spared from annihilation. We can relieve ourselves, quiet down and investigate the circumstance all the more rapidly in light of the fact that we have not expanded the science of wrath. We can start to see the blunders of our own specific manners, picking up, developing and improving therefore. We are additionally ready to think and make sense of what steps should be taken so as to rectify the circumstance. It is everything great!

So as to turn into an ace of discretion, practice We can alleviate ourselves; keeping your mouth shut in minor, ordinary episodes when you need to "answer back," counter or have the final word. As you show signs of improvement and better at this expertise, you will wind up prepared to deal with greater difficulties, until at last you will have the option to keep your mouth shut in the exact instant you are injured, regardless of how harmed you feel. And after that you will satisfy the expressions of Proverbs: "Who is a tough individual? One who has restraint!"

Redefining Perspectives

Aren't connections only a breeze! Said nobody, ever. Let's be honest, we are intricate animals and when we work together with another mind boggling animal we can deliver a rainbow of bright and disorganized outcomes. Getting to the meaningful part of unwinding that coupledom is no simple procedure and the last snap, well it constantly will in general leave an imprint. Our life can truly feel like the crude skin abandoned after the savage ripping off of a mortar — we as a whole know the sensation.

What however, after the tempest of parting has settled? Amidst connections, we bond, we mate and in some cases we even make (other little people) thus as we go separate ways, what of those subtleties? Huge or little, the things we do together all exude with vitality and a mental and once in a while physical result (kids, home... things). Isolating our time and our things to provide food for the remanence of a relationship is the most exceedingly awful sort of maths on the planet... Who gets what and when? It is regularly difficult and constantly precarious.

The thing with us people is that we will in general place a colossal measure of significance on our connections; we endeavor to mate for life and we always remember we've's loved ones, regardless of how it 'so occurred'. The issue is, a lot of connections do not length the eternity course of events and between the underlying tornado of profoundly charged feeling and the unfolding of the real world; offering your life to someone else is truly bleeding hard. The thing is, when love blurs and connections separate, we have options, we can pick how to respond and even proceed to make companionships from the most fierce and sharp of partitions. It is difficult, however it is so advantageous and if there are kids amidst a separation, at that point it is everything the more imperative to pick a co-child rearing game plan that breeds regard and reasonableness; no tyke has the right to be stuck in the middle of two warring grown-ups.

Connections arrive at an end for a wide range of reasons and a portion of those reasons can be forcefully terrible; disloyalty is a noteworthy player with respect to reasons for separation and no uncertainty, finding a kinship borne from such a circumstance is now and again incomprehensible. If you do not have youngsters then there is no genuine should be companions with a miscreant, yet if you do have children... Well, it is a hard trudge, yet it is possible and advantageous; to make something that shields your kids from the drop out of a split. Pardoning is one of the hardest yet most compensating things and if it implies harmony for your family, at that point it is the best approach to push ahead.

Discovering some shared view makes for a decent start when moving toward another point of view on connections. Where there was once love, there are recollections and those mean something when you attempt to find out a companionship subsequent to parting. Concentrating on the great and the positive can open up a universe of chances to be companions with an ex and really, the commonality without the sex or closeness has been known to make lifelong kinships. Rethinking your association with somebody you once adored needn't be an errand or a weight.

Anyway, how would we approach rethinking a relationship? Three Cs...

Thought — having sympathy truly encourages us to interface. We probably will not comprehend or even concur with somebody's activities or point of view, yet attempting to stroll from their perspective for a moment is an absolute necessity in pushing ahead.

Correspondence — numerous couples quit conveying during their relationship and it is simply after that they can reconnect and really hear each out other.

Bargain — compromising with some place with regards to reconnecting with an ex makes for a marginally less crabby beginning. There is an incredible saying in such manner, "Do not anticipate even more a man (or lady) than he (or she) is ready or ready to give." Keeping desires reasonable and being transparent with an ex can ingrain trust and regard just as setting up limits so everybody knows where they stand.

As far as evidence, I am it. My ex and I are currently great companions and bringing up our little girl together while we're not together is ending up being loaded with happiness. Making it to the Nativity together, putting on a splendid birthday end of the week for her and being there as a group for her is our sole need however the advantages of hanging out and having a snicker are certainly a reward as well. In a New York Times Modern Love section titled "Joyfully Ever, After We Split," Wendy Paris subtleties the advancement of her association with her better half through the separation procedure and how isolating united them.

Gwynny and Chris from Coldplay went separate ways with their popular articulation, 'cognizant uncoupling' which, at the time appeared to be fairly dubious (and sounded a bit self important) however in all actuality, it is actually what's going on.

Uncoupling with beauty and pushing ahead as companions... The present day, 'cheerfully ever after.'

Listen to Others

Generally, in all connections there is one individual who talks and one who tunes in. Be that as it may, is the audience truly tuning in?.

The objective of profound listening is to get data, comprehend an individual or a circumstance, and experience delight. Undivided attention is tied in with settling on a cognizant choice to hear what individuals are stating. It is tied in with being totally centered around others—their words and their messages—without being occupied.

It is been said that one of the most widely recognized reasons why individuals see advisors is to have their accounts heard. So as to have your story heard, you need an audience. Tuning in and sympathy abilities are the signs of good communicators, pioneers, and advisors. Listening aptitudes can be adapted, however actually, a few people simply will in general be preferred audience members over others.

The significance of tuning in relational connections cannot be overemphasized. One examination demonstrated that there are two different kinds of tuning in: "tuning in to comprehend" and "tuning in to react." Those who "tune in to comprehend" have more prominent fulfillment in their relational connections than others. While individuals may figure they may tune in to comprehend, what they're truly doing is holding on to react.

Furthermore, when people attempt to "fix" other individuals, they are frequently reacting to their very own need to impact. A similar report demonstrated that couples who have experienced treatment together are better listeners because they can directly apply advice to their relationships. It is been said that ladies as a rule need to be heard, and men need to fix or react.

As indicated by clinicians, dynamic or profound listening is at the core of each sound relationship. It is additionally the best method to realize development and change. The individuals who are heard will in general be increasingly open, progressively majority rule in their ways, and are regularly less guarded. Great audience members cease from making decisions, and give a sheltered domain and holder for speakers.

By listening cautiously when somebody talks, we're revealing to them that we care about what they're stating. It is additionally imperative to recollect that listening is infectious. When we tune in to other people, at that point chances are they will be progressively disposed to hear us out.

Fortunately we can figure out how to be better audience members; notwithstanding, listening takes practice. The more we do it, the better we get at it, and the more constructive our relational connections will be.

Here are a few hints for improving as an audience:

Notice the speaker's tone and enunciation.

Develop sympathy.

Abstain from making decisions.

Rehash in your very own words what somebody has let you know (compassionate reflection).

Recognize that you are tuning in by gesturing or saying "Uh-huh."

Put yourself inside the brain of the speaker.

Focus on non-verbal communication.

Investigate others' eyes when they're talking.

Focus on the sentiments related with the words.

Once in a while outline others' remarks when given the opportunity.

Tune in for importance.

To turn into a compelling communicator, you have to figure out how to listen the same amount of as you have to figure out how to talk. Shockingly, a great many people center more around the talking than they do on the tuning in. Regardless of whether in a one-on-one discussion or a gathering meeting or homeroom, concentrating on what others are stating enables you to introduce yourself all the more adequately. When you listen effectively, you likewise find out additional.

Check out the room during a talk, introduction, or break room. The indications of individuals not listening are all over the place. A few people put on a clear gaze that must be portrayed as their "screen-saver face" (in the expressions of one of my associates). You recognize what that screen-saver face resembles: it is that clear gaze where the eyes are dull and looking vacantly into no place and the face has definitely no demeanor on it by any stretch of the imagination. You'll additionally notice individuals in a gathering or group of spectators who do not take a gander at the speaker by any stretch of the imagination. Actually, they look wherever else.

They mess with their pencil or longingly look at their mobile phone or even attempt to sneak a look at its screen. If there is a window in the room they gaze at the sky, regardless of whether the view is only that of the neighboring place of business. An incredible speaker may charm even the most headstrong group of spectators part. The normal speaker, partner, companion, or relative may experience serious difficulties getting the look of the collected audience members who do not have a clue how to rehearse essential listening aptitudes.

If we are the speakers, we need others to tune in. So for what reason cannot a considerable lot of us play out the support backward? It is conceivable that internet based life are making numerous individuals lose their centering capacity. Generally, the normal audience requires a shift in incitement after around 20 minutes. Be that as it may, with quick fire messages coming wherever from Facebook to Twitter to push notifications from web based games, numerous individuals require a shift in incitement after maybe as short as 15 seconds. Except if you have that magnetic touch, you will experience considerable difficulties battling the consideration shortfalls of your crowd.

The issue with poor audience members is not just that they are seen as impolite yet that they pass up significant information. Investigations of the destructive impact of performing multiple tasks on understudy learning demonstrate that understudies who messaged on their cellphones, messaged, refreshed their Facebook status, and sent texts had less fortunate evaluations than the individuals who tuned in to addresses without diversion. As indicated by the "psychological bottleneck hypothesis," proposed by clinician Alan Welford in 1967, you can just process such a great amount of data on the double before your learning begins to endure.

Coming back to the inconsiderateness point of poor tuning in, individuals who do not listen likewise appear to have less fortunate social abilities when all is said in done. In an examination led in Louisiana found that understudies low in the quality they identified as "dynamic empathic tuning in" had lower scores on a social abilities stock. Being a poor audience is related with more unfortunate social and enthusiastic affectability. This was a correlational report, obviously, so we cannot decide causality. There may likewise be a third (or more) factor influencing both tuning in and social abilities. These qualifications aside, the outcomes are captivating.

Another qualification is the way this was an undergrad test, and as a matter of fact not agent of the populace. In any case, one could contend that it is especially inconvenient for individuals to pick up listening aptitudes when they are in the rising adulthood period of advancement. The social aptitudes you learn in your late youngsters and mid 20s remain with you all through life and can impact the nature of your life. If you do not build up your social aptitudes in your initial grown-up years, you'll have a harder time getting a new line of work, a sentimental partner, and an encouraging group of people you'll require as you progress through adulthood. You may even be an increasingly successful sales rep, if that is the profession you choose to seek after.

Validation

When we consider what we can do to sustain our relationship, we regularly consider physical assets. Get her precious stone hoops. Take her out to a rich supper. Shock him by wearing provocative unmentionables. Purchase blooms and chocolate. Take a sentimental excursion together. While these things surely will not hurt your relationship (by any stretch of the imagination!), they aren't really the most grounded approaches to associate with your adored one.

The more profound part has more to do with how you collaborate together as opposed to what you do together. It is called validation. Reliable, keen validation of your partner's musings and sentiments is the best thing you can accomplish for your relationship.

Recall when you felt truly comprehended. Maybe it was a minding instructor in evaluation school who appeared to know precisely the best thing to state when you were disturbed. Perhaps it is your companion who dropped everything when you called with energizing news and was anxious to share your delight. Recollect the last time you truly felt heard, comprehended, and tuned in to. It is an amazing inclination, would it say it is not?

Validation in your relationship is a similar thought. It implies that when your partner enlightens you concerning their day, or offers their sentiments, you remain with them at the time, respecting their experience. You join their reality and see things from their perspective. It is a method for demonstrating you comprehend and acknowledge their contemplations and emotions similarly as they may be. Research has demonstrated that having these kinds of collaborations with your partner helps your partner feel less annoyed and less powerless, though negating practices do the inverse; they make your partner feel scrutinized, rejected, or disdain from you.

Connections that are the best are those where the two partners share their internal world with each other - their genuine considerations, sentiments and wants - and where their partner, thus, can truly hear them. When you share an approving style of communicating together, you assemble trust and closeness. These are the bonds that make connections last.

While the idea of validation may appear to be basic, it can now and then be somewhat dubious to execute. Envision your partner gets back home and reveals to you they are irate in light of the fact that they discovered they have to work over the occasion end of the week. What is your first response? A large number of us would feel defensive of our life partner, or steamed at the circumstance, and have the common desire to attempt to help or fix the circumstance. You may offer exhortation on the most proficient method to tackle the issue. While it naturally feels supportive to give proposals, this can feel refuting to your partner. Your partner may not be searching for assistance with an answer - they most likely have effectively attempted to discover approaches to take care of the issue, and may feel considerably increasingly disappointed in hearing exhortation, regardless of how great your expectation.

So how would you viably tune in to and approve your partner? There are a couple of key parts to help direct your discussions.

1. Pose inquiries. If your partner introduces an issue or difficult circumstance to you, attempt to discover progressively about how they are feeling and what they need by asking open-finished inquiries. "What do you wish would occur?" "What was your response to that?" "How are you feeling about things currently?" Gently posing inquiries to clarify their experience can be

exceptionally gratifying for them. It demonstrates you give it a second thought and need to truly tune in.

2. Recognizing and tolerating is the following stage in validation. This implies you recognize what they've said or what they are feeling. You may state, "I can see you are vexed about this," or "You appear to be disheartened" because of their report about working throughout the end of the week. Instead of attempting to brighten your partner up, you permit them space to be disturbed.

3. Show you get it. Utilize approving explanations, for example, "I would feel that way, as well," or "It sounds good to me that you would feel that way given the conditions" to tell them you see why they feel the manner in which they do. You can likewise indicate validation with non-verbal, for example, giving them an embrace if they feel desolate, making them some tea if they feel jumpy, or giving them space if they need time to think.

4. Careful listening is the main part of validation. This implies you truly focus on what your partner is stating. As difficult as it may be, suspend your very own decisions and responses to the circumstance or theme. Incidentally let go of the need to prompt, change, help or fix the circumstance. Your own musings are set aside for later; your center, rather, is on your partner's present involvement. Show you are tuning in by halting what you are doing (shutting the PC, killing the TV), going to confront them, gesturing your head, and looking as they talk.

5. Approving doesn't approach concurring. A significant qualification is that you can acknowledge your partner's sentiments, however it doesn't mean you have to concur with them. For example, state that you head out to see a motion picture together. Subsequently, you examine your musings about the film. Your partner thought that it was engaging and interesting, while

you thought that it was exhausting and unsurprising. You may approve their perspective by saying, "It seems like you truly appreciated the film. It wasn't my top choice, yet I can tell that you had a ton of fun watching it." In this model, you are recognizing your partner's delight in something, without having a similar supposition.

At last, it is about the manner in which you collaborate together, significantly more so than what you do together. Also, it can have a significant effect in your relationship.

Chapter 4 – Break the Patterns

Denial

A great many people have an assortment of self-sabotaging practices that keep them from manifesting the life that they need. The initial phase in beating self-sabotaging practices is to initially remember them. One of the most dominant self-sabotaging practices is refusal.

Refusal is a barrier system that releases uneasiness and enthusiastic distress. By denying there is an issue we do not need to feel terrible about the way that there is an issue. Sadly this doesn't tackle anything or improve our lives. It just hides our issues where no one will think to look. They're still there. As yet worrying us and as yet holding us up.

Sometimes we deny our own well being when we fail to acknowledge and tend to a problem currently affecting us. Tragically when it turns into the obvious issue at hand, something we never again can deny, it turns into an issue considerably more difficult to determine than had we recognized it and confronted it when it previously showed up.

One type of denial is denying that our practices are really self-sabotaging. For instance, when we are late for an arrangement we may disclose to ourselves that it will not make any difference, that the reason we give will be acknowledged and that there will not be any negative results. However, this typically is not valid. When we are late for arrangements or do not get back to individuals in time, it will end up ruining your reputation over time and you will be unable to recovert he same respect they once had for you.

Living in the Past

Living before and not recognizing what would be inevitable is a type of forswearing. Regardless of whether you figure pot ought to be authorized and whether you figure gay marriage ought to be sanctioned, what would be inevitable is that these things will one day all around happen and to deny this and battle this is extremely a gigantic exercise in futility, vitality and assets that could best be spent somewhere else.

Another type of refusal is denying that pardoning, acknowledgment and love have the ability to move mountains. The vast majority accept that outrage and hostility are the best approach to take care of issues. In the short run this may appear to be the situation however over the long haul they are most certainly not. Love is a phenomenal power that can change. At the point when two individuals are battling with one another, if one individual can transcend the war zone and express obvious genuine acknowledgment, pardoning and love, it generally can release all the cynicism and reestablish harmony in the relationship.

A great many people imagine that pardoning is an indication of weakness. They do not accept that the quiet will acquire everything of importance. This is refusal. Pardoning is an impression of incredible quality and individual power. Survival of the fittest will one day demonstrate to be survival not of the physically fittest yet of the profoundly fittest: the individuals who decide not to battle and rather demand finding quiet goals.

We harm ourselves with disavowal and in different ways also in light of the fact that at an oblivious level we are loaded up with blame, disgrace and self-hatred. At an oblivious level, we accept we are undeserving and shameful of joy, wellbeing and achievement, and that our intuitive personality, accepting what we are ourselves at an oblivious level, accepting that we merit discipline and not compensate, manifests in reality that "truth" by making us do things that impede us and produce disappointment.

Accusing Others and Seeing Ourselves as Victims

Shakespeare once expressed, "The shortcoming dear Brutus lies not in our stars yet ourselves that we are subordinates." So one type of forswearing would feel that the issue lies outside of ourselves and that we are casualties of a threatening, tumultuous universe out of our control, instead of us being the prime movers of our destiny.

This is an extremely amazing type of forswearing, accusing other individuals and conditions for our difficulties. For instance when we rear end and get into an auto crash we tend to consider it a mishap when it is really the consequence of our misguided thinking and we will in general accuse the vehicle before us for halting unexpectedly.

This is regular to accuse others and not assume liability for our activities. Customarily when couples battle, one partner will accuse the other partner, expressing that "You irritated me. You made me toss the toaster against the divider. You made me shout at you. You made me hit you. If you hadn't irritated me; if you hadn't pushed my catches; if you hadn't considered me that name; if you hadn't incited me, at that point I wouldn't have acted that way." Denial for this situation is the forswearing of possession. It doesn't make a difference if we are incited. We have a decision to carry on effectively and respectably or not and if we do not, and do not let it out then we are trying to claim ignorance.

Forswearing is normal with drunkards and addicts. "If I simply have one beverage it will not generally matter. I'll have the option to deal with it - it will not grow into a difficult issue." Alcoholics and addicts reveal to themselves this in spite of having a background marked by one beverage or one medication hit growing into a major issue.

Another type of refusal with respect to liquor and medications is that individuals generally persuade themselves that other individuals do not have the foggiest idea when they are high. This is typically never the case. The vast majority can tell when other individuals are impaired.

We are willfully ignorant when we misuse other individuals and disclose to ourselves that they'll get over it, they're not going to leave us. For the most part, at some point or another, they do, and when they do there is frequently a lot of no problem, an excessive amount of developed disdain and outrage for the relationship to be fixed.

We are trying to claim ignorance when we continue putting off legitimate eating routine and exercise. The disavowal part is not that we are denying these are significant activities however that it will not one day get up to speed with us and put us in the grave rashly. We deny the long haul outcomes of our activities.

Shooting the Messenger

When somebody reveals to us something we would prefer not to hear or manage, we discover approaches to assault them and refute them with the goal that we do not need to recognize that they've made a valid statement. We may disclose to them that "You do it, as well." And so this enables us to preclude the significance from claiming us getting our very own home all together paying little heed to how other individuals carry on.

Seeing someone when we tell our partner that "I do not have any issue. I needn't bother with outrage the board. You are the one with the issue not me. You are the person who needs treatment not me," this is disavowal in spades and is a certain flame indicator of a relationship that will never mend and will in all probability one day crumble. This is another case of shooting the delivery person.

Another type of forswearing is classified "scorn before examination," which means we prejudge and dismiss a thought without first assessing it to decide whether it may have legitimacy. "That is not getting down to business." "It is an exercise in futility." These are opinionated refusals that have no premise in all actuality since we really haven't took a gander at the information.

Another type of forswearing is "doing likewise and anticipating different outcomes." Some individuals allude to this as craziness.

When we are told something that is valid that we would prefer not to hear or manage and we search out individuals who will yes us and bolster our position, this is refusal. Because we can discover a lot of individuals who disclose to us we're correct doesn't mean we're correct.

"I'm just joking" is a type of refusal. When we express something to someone that is frightful and they respond adversely, we retreat and guarantee that "I was just joking." Sometimes it is not refusal, we realize that we weren't joking and that we were making a brutal point, yet in many cases we con ourselves into accepting that we truly were just joking, we were just prodding, we implied no genuine mischief and that the individual was in effect excessively delicate. This keeps us from taking a gander at our conduct dispassionately and rectifying it.

So if self-damage and forswearing are simply the aftereffect of blame, disgrace and hating, at that point the best approach to end self-harm and refusal is to adore ourselves and pardon ourselves. The best approach to adore ourselves and pardon ourselves is to cherish others, excuse others and be of administration to other people. The more we do this, the more we send the message to our intuitive personality that we are great, adoring creatures who merit satisfaction and achievement, and the more the subliminal personality shifts its motivation. It quits murmuring pessimistic messages in our ears, it quits urging us to take part in self-sabotaging practices, and it encourages us to pull in constructive individuals and conditions in our lives that will remunerate as opposed to rebuffing.

Low Self-Esteem

Low self-esteem and cynicism can make it difficult to acknowledge obligation and useful analysis, which can upset you from circumstances and furthermore keep you from taking on new challenges; therefore, blocking you from having satisfying encounters in life. It can likewise destroy significant connections. Low self-esteem, which influences our feelings, our considerations, and conduct, just as presentations how we see and associate with ourselves as well as other people, can happen for some, reasons, including dissatisfaction from individuals you esteem, placing your self-worth in conditions that are out of your control, which when they do not go the manner in which you need makes you feel like a disappointment, and some psychological issue, for example, marginal character issue and wretchedness.

With regards to poor self-esteem, there are a few things you can do to help beat it and be the individual you were intended to be, including:

Give Back

Giving, volunteering, and helping other people that are less blessed, not just helps take the concentration off your own issues, however it additionally makes you feel great realizing you are helping other people.

Deal with Yourself

Basic things like scrubbing down, brushing your hair, wearing clean garments, eating right, and practicing consistently help you rest easy thinking about yourself. Concentrates additionally demonstrate that creation your living space agreeable, spotless and appealing likewise help improve your disposition.

Encircle Yourself with the Right People

Low self-esteem as a rule starts right off the bat in life on account of disliking specialist figures. For example, if you were always informed that you do not measure up or you were scrutinized for all that you did, it can keep you from developing into a certain grown-up with a positive self-picture.

Try not to Compare Yourself to Others

Psychotherapists caution that correlations just lead to a negative self-picture, which can prompt poor self-esteem, stress, and tension that thus can destroy your work, connections, and physical and psychological well-being.

Become acquainted with Yourself/Become Your Own Best Friend

In spite of your differences, you are profitable and have the right to like yourself. In this way, invest energy alone and set aside effort to become more acquainted with yourself, which will enable you to find where you are one of a kind, unique, and commendable, which will enable you to increase a superior valuation for yourself. You can likewise take a stab at making a rundown of your accomplishments and qualities to help yourself to remember your accomplishments, and after that audit it at whatever point you need self-esteem and need to rest easy thinking about yourself.

This is additionally an extraordinary time to pinpoint and go up against any negative perspectives that you have about yourself.

Rehash Positive Affirmations

Similarly as negative attestations, for example, you are inept, can be accepted, they can likewise be unbelieved. Accordingly, analysts propose that you rehash positive insistences that you need to accept about yourself day by day to help get you back in good shape to a period before you had low-self esteem. Indeed, inquire about demonstrates that positive insistences can even help decrease side effects of gloom and the sky is the limit from there.

Recognize Where You Need Change

We as a whole have issues; notwithstanding, if you do not perceive and recognize where you need change, it can keep you trapped in an endless cycle of poor self-esteem, which will just deteriorate the more you attempt to keep running from it. Rather, become mindful of and recognize where you need change and afterward set forth the push to improve it. You can even enroll a decent companion or relative for help.

You ought to likewise end up mindful when you are excessively reproachful of yourself, and afterward advise yourself that these are not certainties, which will help you stay away from negative feelings that can prompt negative self-talk.

At last, individuals with a positive self-gratefulness are available to progress and increasingly significant encounters, which means they do not depend on outer fortifications, for example, status or salary, for self-worth, which empowers them to encounter more joy and have a great time life. In this manner, be aware of who you permit into your life just as the conditions you permit to manage your self-worth. You ought to likewise be careful to deal with yourself, including activity and eating ideal, to help keep your both your body and your mind sound.

Compliance

This post has been extremely difficult to compose. Not on the grounds that pondering back my relationship works up an entire arrangement of feelings: outrage; sharpness; disappointment; upset and now alleviation, yet mainly in light of the fact that it is extremely difficult to articulate that time. It is difficult to verbalize, in a way that doesn't make me sound sensational and powerless, what my relationship resembled.

If there are two key exercises that I have learned they are that:

Dangerous connections can sneak up on anybody.

My ex and I were as one for a long time. In spite of the fact that there were unobtrusive pieces of information at an early stage, I was heedless to them and could never have anticipated that our relationship would turn out the manner in which it did.

Psychological mistreatment, and I do delay at calling this maltreatment, can be unpretentious and practically difficult to analyze and seldom unmistakable to those outside of the relationship.

This drove me to address myself and to accept that everything was my deficiency and in my very own head.

Here are a few highlights of my relationship:

His analysis was interminable.

Regularly it was simply little things: he didn't care for my nails to be excessively long or painted in light of the fact that "they look like paws"; I was not talkative and active enough with companions at gatherings; I ought to accomplish more exercise; we should look for his sister's recommendation on beautifying our home since "she has an extremely inventive eye". She may well have an innovative eye, yet this was our home, our home, my home and my home. He said that I was passionate and hormonal after labor and not equipped for settling on a reasonable choice. He demanded addressing my mom, inferring that she was fit for the consistent idea that I could not summon.

In open things were altogether different. Perfect suitor was on structure "Pen is an exceptionally gifted craftsman", "Pen was unemotional during work".

Truth be told understanding it now it sounds snobby and insignificant, yet when the little day by day evaluate develops and you feel like each easily overlooked detail you do could utilize improvement in your partner's eyes you are not being esteemed as an equivalent, and you are surely not being adored unequivocally.

He utilized his 'feelings' to control me.

My ex said that he would "fault, resent and dislike me for the remainder of our lives" if I didn't agree to a Catholic dedicating for our child. These words, his face and the recreation center that we were strolling in at the time will be always engraved in my brain. He at that point cried. He said that our child must be dedicated a Catholic since his dad had changed over to Catholicism on his passing bed fourteen years back.

Yet, my ex never goes to Church, he is a divorcé who hitched ten years back to get his now ex a visa to remain in the UK, we lived together and had an infant without any father present. These are not the activities of a Catholic. In any case, I could not challenge my ex on this point since I felt regretful about his Dad's passing. I could not address him during his overflowing of misery.

He put down my convictions.

My ex yelled that my absence of religion was 'a vacuum', 'a void' in me and that I could always be unable to interface or to completely comprehend being otherworldly and to accept.

Presently do not misunderstand me, it is incredible when our partners can challenge us into intriguing discourses and give us better approaches for taking a gander at the world. This is the thing that I need from a relationship. It is not incredible when they make you feel senseless, or moronic, or little, or deficient, or they reliably attempt to alter your perspective on something critical to you and which you have faith in. It deteriorates when they intentionally disregard your perspectives, over-rule you as well as go despite your good faith.

Receptiveness to new experience is incredible, however a controlling partner doesn't consider it to be a two-way road, and just needs you to figure increasingly as they do.

He made me so tired of contending that I needed to yield.

I stay away from struggle. I know this. I have to show signs of improvement at it. I got depleted rapidly from any 'talk' so would yield. Consistence was simpler... until it got to an issue where his wants were so absolutely inconsistent with my conviction framework and his dangers were obvious to such an extent that I could not consent any more. I needed to end it.

He had a terrifying temper.

He never hit me, yet he would regularly hit his clench hand against the table directly before where I was sitting. If we were in the vehicle he would quicken hard so the riggings were shouting and after that pummel his foot on the brake. He previously did this from the get-go in the relationship the morning after I had would not get in the vehicle with him since he had been drinking. That was a piece of information in those days, a sign which I overlooked. He did this in January a year ago while our infant, Cygnet, was in the back of the vehicle. By at that point, it was excessively.

I am out of the relationship now. All things considered, I am out of the relationship in a sentimental sense. We will have a co-child rearing relationship as long as we both will live.

What panics me the most presently, is that I will not have the option to pass judgment on whether the following individual I meet is a comparative sort of controlling person. I realize that our control/consistence dynamic crawled up on me. The harmful idea of our relationship snuck up on me. By what means will I see it coming?

This is the reason I do not figure I can even consider getting into another relationship yet. I do not have the confidence in my own quality of brain to have the option to identify and follow up on the signs.

I do not have a clue about that I ever will.

One of the most well-known and unsafe propensities that I see in couples and even long haul relationships is the prevalent conduct of advising your partner what they need to hear as opposed to what you need, need, think and feel. When we oblige our partner as opposed to connect on a genuine and valid level, it constructs a marriage with precarious stilts that can topple whenever.

Satisfying, accommodating people and consistence are common. So for what reason is this propensity so unavoidable?

There are numerous elements why we tell others what we think they need to hear, particularly our partner.

- Danger of being rebuked

- Dread of dismissal

- Do not have the foggiest idea how to define limits

- Shirking of awkward sentiments

- We like satisfying others, particularly those we adore

- We do not have the foggiest idea what we truly need so we come

- Maintain a strategic distance from strife or a contention

- Scared by another's responses

It is only simple—until it is most certainly not.

It may not generally be anything but difficult to react with a certifiable and fair reaction, yet nobody can make a flourishing and upbeat relationship without genuineness. Trust is based on genuineness.

There are no solid connections without every individual being consistent with themselves first. When we go along or please for a portion of the above reasons, it is improbable that we are flourishing in our relationship. Why? Since we start feeling imperceptible like we do not make a difference to the next individual despite the fact that we're the ones making that experience. It is likewise implausible that our needs or objectives get cultivated—at any rate not so quick. Nor do we get the help or delight of sharing the voyage of our development and yearnings if we're continually agreeing to our partner.

When I was first hitched, I made every effort to abstain from disquieting my better half. In addition to the fact that I sought to satisfy him (before myself), yet I additionally pushed down my wants and supplanted them with his. At that point when we had kids, my days were loaded up with fulfilling everybody. Despite the fact that my conduct gave off an impression of being chipping away at the surface, inside, I felt empty, and each trade appeared to be somewhat of a trick. Furthermore, despite the fact that individuals saw me as a friendly, kind individual, I understood that genuine thoughtfulness needed to likewise be benevolent and wanting to me.

Related perusing: Why Being a People Pleaser Damages Relationships—and What to Do About It!

There is a Difference among Kindness and Pleasing

Consideration is not thoughtful except if it is additionally kind to YOU. Individuals who look to satisfy others without considering their very own needs take a major slip up for a few reasons.

1) If we do not appear in our associations with what we think, want, and need, there is no legitimate correspondence. When we retain our fact from others, people around us are following up on incorrect, fragmented, or unhelpful data that has results regardless of whether they are indistinct at the time.

2) Even if you think you have a quite smart thought of who your partner is, I would rather not break it to you—you are not a mind reader! Perhaps the greatest grumbling I get notification from the two people in an affection relationship is that their partner attempts to reveal to them what they think or how they feel, or even attempt to talk for them. We cannot realize what is happening in someone else regardless of to what extent we've been as one. Intriguing suppositions without getting limits closeness, comprehension, and association. Thinking we KNOW what our partner thinks or feels acts like a messy channel that stains and foils important discussions. This propensity for expecting likewise flares contentions.

3) When an individual is an inactive member in a relationship, the wellbeing and essentialness of the association cannot bloom since it is unjust. A lot of falls on one individual and the relationship does not have the uniqueness that could be made by the full commitment and move of the two individuals. Also, here and there, the relationship will even sink into turning into the meaning of that word everybody severely dislikes: codependent.

4) When we fully trust our partner's pledge and accept what they guide us to be valid yet they are retaining their genuine emotions, inclinations or aversions, love's potential is repudiated and the shallowness takes from conceivable outcomes. One minute, one experience can transform us! One keen discussion can shift how we see the world and one another. Try not to pass up this beautiful association by telling your partner what you think they need to hear rather than what you truly mean and need to state.

5) Whenever an individual concurs with untruthfulness or to assuage, the two individuals in the relationship leave a circumstance or discussion with different deductions and comprehension, which once in a while has positive results. These trades will in general

make ready for misconception in future connections. It very well may be as straightforward as telling your partner that their spaghetti sauce is delectable when you truly believe it is excessively harsh or sweet.

It is every individual's obligation to step up to the plate bat for their very own needs in a relationship.

Pleasers debilitate themselves and the relationship by putting their partner at the disservice of blended messages or negligible understanding. Consistence and exploitative reactions are ruinous on the grounds that they just make a fantasy of association or understanding.

In solid and develop connections, we please others most when we are consistent with ourselves.

At exactly that point would we be able to give and get from a free and cherishing space.

Control

Seeing someone, there is normally somewhat of a battle for who has the advantage. With control issues over who will be the more prevailing figure, a little clash of the genders may begin. Ladies regularly need to demonstrate their freedom and demonstrate that they are similarly as solid as men. In the interim, men need the power and high ground as well. So here are a few different ways that you can be in charge or addition control without giving the relationship a chance to endure subsequently.

Instructions to Be in Control in a Relationship

Set Boundaries

You likely have your very own arrangement of principles that fall inside your customary range of familiarity, so it is imperative to keep a portion of those when you are seeing someone. If you do not have limits and you feel the requirement for more control, attempt and set a few. Know your points of confinement and talk them obviously to your partner. Furthermore, ensure your partner realizes that no methods no and approves your choice with steady fair articulations.

Have Self Respect

Nobody else will have regard for you if you do not have it for yourself. Seeing someone, regard is basic, so demonstrate your partner you regard yourself. Take care by they way you talk about yourself, how you handle power and how you see your character. This will all be reverberated back by your partner.

Keep up Your Independence

Continuously try to demonstrate your partner you are your very own individual. It is beneficial to have your very own side interests and companions to invest your energy with outside of the relationship. This is a decent method for how to be in charge in a relationship since it demonstrates that you are alright with yourself.

Demonstrate Your Confidence

Having certainty is alluring, and if you have faith in yourself, at that point being in charge ought to be simpler. Demonstrate your partner that you merit the best. This kind of certainty will enable you to have more power in a relationship. If you are battling with certainty, attempt to recall what is most essential to you and that you are significant and meriting. At that point, radiate this in your relationship to help increase a touch of control.

Attempt to Be Unavailable

Without messing around, ensure your partner realizes you have a life outside of the relationship. This is particularly significant in the first place with the goal that they do not think you are excessively poor. Demonstrate to them that you cherish yourself, that you can finish yourself without them, and that your relationship adds to the fantastic life you as of now have. This will help you in making sense of how to be in charge in a relationship.

Act Consistent with Your Words

There are numerous ways for how to be in charge in a relationship. If you need to be paid attention to additional by your partner and increase more control, at that point try to finish your words. Your partner will feel the difference and regard you more if you act steady with your remarks. Likewise, you need to try to finish and act when you are having a contention with your partner. If you state there will be sure repercussions, at that point ensure you stand firm. Your partner will not pay attention to you if you generally give in against your promise. It works the equivalent for keeping guarantees; make a point to be straightforward and do what you state.

Use Silence During Conflict

At the point when your partner is harming you somehow or another or being out of line, attempt to remain quiet instead of demonstrating that you lose control of your feelings so rapidly. Your partner will acknowledge they do not have as much control over you if you do not respond so rapidly to clashes. If you are considering how to be in charge in a relationship, attempt to get things done in different ways if it is not working. By taking the peaceful, quiet approach, you will find your partner napping, which may help shift the power balance.

Utilize Your Voice

Make some noise and be clear about what you need out of your partner. If they regard you, it will mean a ton to them that you are forthright and legitimate. By imparting obviously, you will demonstrate that you are in charge. This will likewise make you feel progressively enabled.

Treat Others How You Want to Be Treated

The great good old brilliant guideline of treating others how you need to be dealt with is a decent method to get regard from your partner. This will likewise enable you to increase some control that you may have lost. It demonstrates that you are responsible for your conduct and decisions and that you pay attention to it.

Try not to Settle for Less

Demonstrate your partner that you are certain and realize what you merit. If one partner can pull off anything, at that point the other's capacity is lost. It is essential to support yourself and hold your ground. Additionally, if something is not working out the manner in which you need, do not be reluctant to leave. Show you have authority over your feelings and decisions.

Try not to Waste Time with Games

A grown-up relationship is one where the control is adjusted, and if you attempt and mess around, at that point you are disturbing the power balance. You likewise would prefer not to date somebody who likes to play and is great at those games since it frequently will prompt them removing control from you. Increase control in your relationship by indicating you do not have to go into a power battle through immature games.

Talk about the Power Struggle

Before you bounce into ends or think the most exceedingly awful, attempt and examine with your partner that you need the control to be increasingly adjusted. Go through models and represent what you expect in the relationship. Offer with your partner that you need to feel that the control is not uneven.

Avoidance

Avoidance behaviors are any moves an individual makes to escape from difficult musings and emotions. These behaviors can happen from numerous points of view and may incorporate activities that an individual does or doesn't do. Individuals with frenzy issue regularly take on avoidance behaviors to evade frightful musings, sentiments of fear, and by and large tension related manifestations.

As an individual managing frenzy and uneasiness, you may as of now be comfortable with carrying on of avoidance. These behaviors can negatively affect numerous parts of your life, including your vocation, connections, and individual interests or leisure activities. You may wind up maintaining a strategic distance from openings for work, get-togethers, and even kinships trying to keep your tension under control.

Perceive When It is Happening

So as to change any maladaptive behavior, you should initially begin getting to be mindful of when it is happening. Toward the part of the arrangement, stop and think about how you occupied with avoidance behaviors consistently. Record any that stick out. You may have seen how you did this in little ways. For instance, maybe you avoided a collaborator since you felt on edge about chatting with him.

When you start to reliably follow your activities, you might be astounded to discover that you are partaking in more avoidance behaviors than you recently suspected.

You may likewise see huge manners by which you occupied with avoidance, for example, taking a different course to work to maintain a strategic distance from interstate driving since it makes you feel restless. Just by endeavoring to see these activities will you be prepared to transform them.

Impacts of Avoidance Behaviors

Beside confining your life, avoidance behaviors frequently have the contrary impact than what is wanted. While in the short run you may encounter an impermanent good feeling, over the long haul, avoidance really prompts expanded tension.

When maintaining a strategic distance from spots, individuals, and occasions, the frenzy sufferer is truly attempting to make tracks in an opposite direction from her sentiments of nervousness. Nonetheless, every time she gets away from these tension actuating considerations and emotions, she is really fortifying them. She is sending the message to herself that the world is a risky spot. At last, she may turn out to be progressively scared of an ever increasing number of improvements, considering the cycle of tension to intensify.

Why Avoidance Coping Creates Additional Stress

Individuals who live with avoidance are frequently denying themselves of numerous encounters, undertakings, and associations. Frenzy related avoidance behaviors might keep you from carrying on with your life without limit. Peruse ahead for certain tips on the most proficient method to diminish your uneasiness related avoidance behaviors.

Discovering Trust and Support

The way to defeating avoidance behaviors is to keep on gradually face what you are maintaining a strategic distance from until it never again has such a hold on you. Obviously, doing so is far actually quite difficult. That is the reason it is prescribed that you do not confront recently maintained a strategic distance from circumstances alone, but instead take part in them with a confided in companion or relative close by.

Tell your companion that the circumstance you are venturing into is normally a wellspring of uneasiness. Have a reinforcement plan prepared should things go sideways. For instance, is going to a huge get-together that you would ordinarily maintain a strategic distance from, talk heretofore about what you'll require if you feel awkward. Set up your adored one to give you space if you should need a couple of minutes alone to deal with your nervousness. Maybe you will caution her that you should leave if manifestations become unmanageable. Notwithstanding your arrangement, ensure your cherished one knows about it so she will recognize what's in store should your tension emerge.

Disclosing Your Panic Disorder to Friends and Family

Note that you never ought to depend on one individual to support your sentiments of nervousness consistently. Thusly, you may incidentally make a shift in avoidance where you become excessively subject to this individual. In the long run, you will need to step into the already avoidances alone. Your adored one may at present be supporting you from a separation, yet it is just when you push ahead alone that you can really defeat your avoidance behaviors.

Create Ways to Cope With Your Anxiety

Your avoidance behaviors rotate around not having any desire to encounter uneasiness or different manifestations of frenzy issue. The best method to move beyond this dread is to learn procedures that will enable you to control your manifestations. Adapting abilities can enable you to hold your nervousness within proper limits and may even help with dealing with your fits of anxiety. Such abilities can be learned through the assistance of a specialist or all alone by utilizing self-help books.

Some basic procedures to help in adapting to uneasiness include:

Dynamic muscle unwinding

Profound breathing activities

Subjective rebuilding

Nervousness following

Expert Help Is Available

Few out of every odd frenzy issue sufferer will encounter avoidance behaviors, notwithstanding, many will find that these issues put unnecessary limitations on their lives. If you are finding that your avoidance behaviors are unmanageable and crazy, it might be an ideal opportunity to look for expert assistance. Getting proficient assistance with your side effects is in no way, shape or form a disappointment on your part. Truth be told, numerous individuals with frenzy issue have discovered that they recuperate snappier through treatment.

Numerous individuals feel on edge in their relationship, in light of the fact that their partner keeps away from enthusiastic closeness. In spite of how baffling the avoidant partner may show up, not all things can be accused on them.

Any relationship contains a dynamic between two individuals, and issues inside the relationship must be inspected with regards to the two partners. To comprehend avoidance with regards to a relationship, we should begin with a rundown of avoidant behaviors.

Identifying Avoidant Behaviors in Your Partner

Here are a few behaviors regularly shown by the "avoidant" partner:

- Not returning writings, messages, or calls

- Overlooking plans, uncommon events, or dates

- Not saying "I adore you" or different articulations of adoration

- Avoiding discussions about further duty, for example, monogamy, commitment, or marriage

- Rejecting or taunting an partner's endeavors to be nearer, or to connect on a more profound level

This behavior can be baffling, and can make the avoidant individual's partner wonder what is "off-base" with the relationship, and whether the avoidant partner even cherishes them by any stretch of the imagination. There are regularly contentions about the relationship, where one partner faults the other for not minding "enough" or demonstrating their affection in specific ways. These battles can undermine the quality of the relationship and dissolve closeness after some time.

For this situation, the avoidant individual's partner is normally thought to be "distracted" or "on edge" in the connection writing.

This implies they can act nosy and controlling when gone up against with their partner's avoidance. The possibility that the avoidant partner doesn't love them or wouldn't like to focus on them completely triggers a frenzy reaction (called connection alarm).

What to do When You Recognize Avoidance in Your Partner

The primary activity when you perceive that your partner is avoidant is to make sense of how your very own behaviors and past issues are adding to the dynamic. It can work with a couple's advisor, yet by and large, a great many people who are intuitively attracted to avoidant partners have had encounters in their initial life where a parent or other key connection figure was relationally repressed.

When they meet an avoidant partner, these individuals intuitively observe an opportunity to at last cause a relationally stunted individual to submit, and be available and mindful. These couples become caught in a follower distancer dynamic, which implies that one partner seeks after the other for closeness, while different pushes away to build enthusiastic separation.

For some, individuals joined forces with avoidant individuals, it tends to be exceptionally valuable to inspect their very own reactions to the avoidant behavior, and make sense of if they are useful or not. For example, messaging your partner multiple times straight to disclose to them how harmed you are that they haven't reacted to you yet is not typically an accommodating behavior. This can make the avoidant individual feel focused, overpowered, and assaulted. So what would it be a good idea for you to do?

Tolerating Your Partner for Who They Are

The way in to a fruitful association with an avoidant partner is to acknowledge what their identity is, while remaining consistent with what you need. This doesn't mean what you need — which may at the time be a steady, progressing content discussion that keeps going 16 waking hours — however what you have to feel like nothing is wrong with the world and sound, which could be an partner who can say "I cherish you," or one who doesn't avoid plans.

If the avoidant partner attempts to react to your essential connection needs, do not be hesitant to part of the arrangement. In any case, if they are attempting to address your issues yet have their very own issues to work through, this may not really flag that things will not work out.

The follower distancer dynamic is normal, and it doesn't need to imply that your relationship is damned. A specialist can enable you to recognize which of the relationship issues are fundamentally because of your frailties, and which are because of your partner's example of passionate avoidance.

Fortify Your Relationship with Couples Therapy

Most relationship issues are, as you may figure, because of the unpredictable transaction between these connection styles, which can frequently be investigated gainfully with a couples instructor. Regardless of whether a cheerful relationship appears to be far away now, numerous issues can be effectively explored with the assistance of an expert.

Recovery Reminders

The facts confirm that affection is unselfish. When we have youngsters, their requirements need to precede our own. We are not going to give our infant a chance to weep for a considerable length of time from appetite in the night since we want to rest when the infant would prefer to be alert and eating. We will drive our kids around to exercises when we are drained or would prefer to accomplish something different. Acting capably as a parent is a piece of loving our kids.

In any case, when we generally put the other first in our grown-up connections, to the detriment of our own wellbeing or prosperity, we might be codependent.

About Codependency

Codependency is a scholarly behavior. We watch the activities of our folks when we are kids. If our mom or father had an issue with limits, was consistently the saint, would never say 'no' to individuals, and had unfortunate approaches to impart, we doubtlessly took in these behaviors and brought them into our private connections.

Youngsters who grow up with relationally stunted guardians likewise are in danger for being codependent. They regularly wind up seeing someone where their partner is relationally stunted, yet they remain in the expectations that they can change the individual. Regardless of what occurs, they will not quit trusting that one day things will be great.

The subliminal expectation is that the other individual will see all the affection we give and be motivated to change. We accept that if we simply hold tight and give our affection, comprehension, and backing, we will at long last get the adoration that we wanted from our folks. This reasoning is damaging if we do not have solid limits that shield us from physical or enthusiastic mischief and sign to our partner that their harsh behavior is not satisfactory.

The most noticeably terrible part is the point at which we do not understand what is happening and keep on living in a cold association since we have never realized what a decent organization resembles. Codependent individuals do not accept that they are deserving of adoration, so they settle for less. Frequently, they end up taking mental, passionate, physical, and even sexual maltreatment from their partner.

Individuals who are codependent frequently search for things outside of themselves to feel much improved.

They structure connections that are not beneficial, hoping to 'fix' the other individual. An individual with codependent propensities may end up in a close association with an individual who has addiction issues that reason them to be relationally repressed. Their partner or they themselves might be obsessive workers or build up some other urgent behavior to maintain a strategic distance from the sentiment of vacancy in the relationship. This is simpler in the present moment than glimpsing inside and managing feelings.

The most effective method to Tell if You are Codependent

If you are seeing someone you think might be codependent, the initial step to freedom is to quit taking a gander at the other and investigate yourself.

If you genuinely state that you concur with the accompanying articulations, you might be codependent.

You will in general love individuals that you can pity and protect.

You feel in charge of the activities of others.

You accomplish more than your offer in the relationship to keep the harmony.

You fear being surrendered or alone.

You feel in charge of your partner's joy.

You need endorsement from others to pick up your own self-worth.

You experience issues acclimating to change.

You experience issues settling on choices and regularly question yourself.

You are hesitant to confide in others.

Your mind-sets are constrained by the contemplations and sentiments of people around you.

Codependency is regularly found in individuals with marginal character issue (BPD), despite the fact that this doesn't mean all individuals with codependency issues additionally meet the criteria for a conclusion of BPD.

The Relationship Between Codependency and Addiction

One of the numerous issues with a codependent relationship is that you might be accidentally empowering an partner's addiction.

In your endeavor to demonstrate your affection by "helping" your partner, you can demoralize that person from looking for the treatment important to get calm.

For instance:

You justify your better half's drinking by saying he has had an unpleasant day or requirements to unwind.

You rationalize when your better half cannot come to social capacities since she is affected by heroin.

You let your sweetheart acquire your remedy narcotics at whatever point he gripes of any minor distress, despite the fact that you are stressed over his developing reliance on the prescription.

You discreetly take on additional obligations around the house or in child rearing your kids on the grounds that your partner is constantly impaired.

You wind up much of the time saying 'sorry' to other people or doing favors to fix connections harmed by your partner's medication or liquor misuse.

You hazard your own monetary future by advancing cash to your partner to cover obligations brought about from substance misuse.

Addiction weakens judgment and basic reasoning aptitudes. This makes it extremely difficult for somebody with a substance use issue to see that the person in question needs assistance. When you make a special effort to keep your partner from encountering the outcomes of substance misuse, you make it more outlandish that the individual will recognize that an issue exists.

Cherishing somebody with a substance use issue can likewise cause your codependent propensities to winding crazy. At the point when your partner is acting whimsically because of medication or liquor misuse, it is anything but difficult to fall back on utilizing codependent behavior in your battle to keep up a feeling of authority over turbulent environment. This makes an endless loop that traps both of you in a dysfunctional and unfortunate relationship.

Recuperating from Codependency

Fortunately codependency is a scholarly behavior, which means it very well may be unlearned. If you cherish your partner and need to keep the relationship, you have to mend yourself as a matter of first importance.

Some sound strides to recuperating your relationship from codependency include:

Start being straightforward with yourself and your partner. Doing things that we would prefer not to do not just burns through our time and vitality, yet it additionally expedites feelings of hatred. Making statements that we do not mean just harms us, since we at that point are carrying on a falsehood. Be straightforward in your correspondence and in communicating your needs and wants.

Stop negative reasoning. Catch yourself when you start to think adversely. If you start to imagine that you have the right to be dealt with seriously, get yourself and change your musings. Be sure and have higher desires.

Try not to think about things literally. It takes a ton of work for a codependent individual not to think about things literally, particularly when in a private relationship. Tolerating the different as they are without attempting to fix or change them is the initial step.

Take breaks. There is nothing amiss with taking a break from your partner. It is beneficial to have companionships outside of your association. Going out with companions takes us back to our inside, helping us to remember who we truly are.

Think about guiding. Get into guiding with your partner. An instructor fills in as an impartial outsider. They can call attention to codependent inclinations and activities among you that you may not know about. Input can give a beginning stage and bearing. Change cannot occur if we do not change.

Depend on companion support. Mutually dependent people Anonymous is a 12-advance gathering like Alcoholics Anonymous that encourages individuals who need to break free of their codependent behavior designs.

Set up limits. The individuals who battle with codependency frequently experience difficulty with limits. We do not have the foggiest idea where our needs start or where the opposite's end. We regularly flourish off blame and feel terrible when we do not put the other first.

Self-Care Is Not Selfish

As you are attempting to break the cycle of codependency, it might appear as though you are being urged to act in way that is selfish and out of line to your partner. This could not possibly be more off-base.

In a sound relationship, the two individuals have full grown characters outside of their time together. They each carry exceptional ascribes to the table—making an association that enables them two to develop and flourish.

Watching a friend or family member battle with medication or liquor addiction is tragic, yet you will not be in any situation to help your partner's addiction treatment except if you set aside a few minutes to address your own emotional wellness needs.

Conclusion

Thank you for making it through to the end of *Codependency Recovery Guide*, let's hope it was informative and able to provide you with all of the tools you need to achieve your goals whatever they may be.

The next step is to like us on social media and spread the word on the relevance of the book to others in difficult relationships.

Finally, if you found this book useful in any way, an honest review is always appreciated!

www.ingramcontent.com/pod-product-compliance
Lightning Source LLC
Chambersburg PA
CBHW060404080526
44583CB00012B/469